MICROSOFT SHAREPOINT

The Most Complete and Updated Guide
to Store, Organize, Share, and Access
Information from Any Device

JAMES HOLLER

Thank You
for your purchase!

SCAN THIS QR CODE BELOW to get your

4 FREE BONUS to boost your productivity **in only 7 days!**

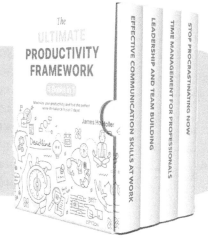

SCAN ME

> BOOK 1: HOW TO SET UP YOUR PERFECT OFFICE AT HOME
> BOOK 2: TIME MANAGEMENT FOR PROFESSIONALS
> BOOK 3: STOP PROCRASTINATING NOW!
> BOOK 4: EFFECTIVE COMMUNICATION SKILLS AT WORK

If you have any questions or feedback feel free to drop me an email
to ✉ info@jamesholler.com

Good work!
Your Teacher,
James

TABLE OF CONTENTS

INTRODUCTION

Hello, fellow explorer! I invite you on a thrilling journey that will change the way you view and interact with one of the most robust tools in today's corporate landscape: Microsoft SharePoint. Over my twelve-year stint as an IT consultant, I have seen the magic that software like SharePoint can weave, transforming the way organizations function. However, despite its prowess, SharePoint often finds itself misunderstood and underutilized. I wrote this book with one primary mission: to pull SharePoint out of the shadows and into the spotlight, illuminating its vast potential and making it accessible to all.

Microsoft SharePoint: The Most Complete and Updated Guide to Store, Organize, Share, and Access Information from Any Device is not just a technical manual; it's an invitation to embark on a quest to discover SharePoint's vast oceans and hidden treasures. It's an expedition into the heart of SharePoint, its growth story, and the limitless opportunities it opens up for increasing productivity and elevating your digital workspace.

This book's objectives are clear and straightforward. Firstly, we aim to dissect SharePoint, delving into every nook and cranny of its features and showing you myriad ways to harness these for better efficiency. We'll take you on a deep dive into SharePoint's intricate architecture, from setting up SharePoint sites to managing workflows. Our aim? To empower you to master this platform.

Secondly, this book pivots on the practical application of SharePoint in your day-to-day life. While the theory is key, applying this knowledge is what truly matters. So, we'll walk side by side through a labyrinth of step-by-step instructions, share the best-kept industry secrets, and, through real-life examples, show you how SharePoint can indeed revolutionize your workspace.

Lastly, with the tech world advancing at breakneck speed, it's crucial to keep abreast of the latest changes. Hence, this book isn't just about SharePoint's present; it's also a telescope into its future. With the most recent updates and informed predictions about prospective trends, we aim to make you a pioneer on the SharePoint journey.

We start by introducing you to the universe of SharePoint before venturing into the specific elements that make it tick: setting it up, understanding its interface, and unlocking the secrets of lists and libraries. We'll take a closer look at SharePoint's document control features, workflows, and automation. Together, we will navigate through SharePoint's security measures, learn to manage permissions, and explore its search and content management abilities.

As we journey deeper, you'll see how seamlessly SharePoint interacts with other tools in the Microsoft Office Suite and learn about the perks of migrating to SharePoint Online. We'll also shed light on valuable tips, best practices, and troubleshooting hacks to keep you ahead in your SharePoint journey. As our expedition concludes, we'll also peek into the future, considering what lies ahead for SharePoint.

Whether you're a veteran professional or a greenhorn venturing into the universe of Microsoft SharePoint, this book is your trusted ally, your compass, and your guide. Let's unlock the power of SharePoint together and revolutionize the way you work.

Here's to a journey of exploration, knowledge, and mastery.

CHAPTER 1

UNDERSTANDING MICROSOFT SHAREPOINT

Microsoft SharePoint is a multifunctional platform that enables individuals and enterprises to collaborate on documents, share them, and manage them in an easy and effective manner. SharePoint was developed by Microsoft. SharePoint, which was developed with the intention of easing the flow of information and decreasing the obstacles that already existed within businesses, has become an indispensable component in a variety of corporate settings. But in order for us to have a complete comprehension of the system, we need to go into its history and investigate its development as well as the advantages it gives to the people who utilize it.

HISTORY AND EVOLUTION OF SHAREPOINT

Since its launch in 2001, Microsoft SharePoint has been subjected to a surprising amount of development since the company first began working on the project. SharePoint was first presented as a content management system for use on intranets; however, it has now evolved into a powerful platform that can be utilized for enterprise collaboration as well as information management. Microsoft has, during the course of its existence, consistently extended and improved the capabilities of SharePoint in order to cater to the ever-evolving requirements of businesses. SharePoint started out as a simple tool for document management and communication, but it has since expanded to offer more advanced capabilities such as customized web components, increased search functionality, workflows, social networking, and connection with other Microsoft products and cloud services. In its early days, SharePoint was primarily used for managing and collaborating on documents. Microsoft has brought enhancements to the user interface, scalability, mobile support, hybrid capabilities, and performance with each iteration of SharePoint, including

SharePoint 2007, 2010, 2013, 2016, and 2019. The introduction of SharePoint Online as a component of the Microsoft 365 suite brought about additional changes to the platform, including the availability of a cloud-based subscription model, the provision of frequent updates, the establishment of the seamless connectivity with the other Microsoft 365 services, and the enhancement of collaboration capabilities. The development and versatility of SharePoint have been demonstrated throughout its history. As a result, this platform has become an indispensable resource for businesses looking to improve their methods of collaboration, document management, and communication.

SharePoint Portal Server 2000

An important turning point in the development of Microsoft's platform for collaboration and document management occurred with the release of SharePoint Portal Server 2000, which was also referred to as SharePoint 2001. It offered businesses a comprehensive solution for the management of their digital assets, encouraged collaboration among teams, and made it easier to share information.

SharePoint Portal Server 2000 was notable for the extensive document management capabilities it offered. This was one of its key selling points. Users were given the ability to construct document libraries, which facilitated the storage, organization, and straightforward access of files by authorized workers. Users were able to monitor changes and revert to earlier revisions of papers thanks to a feature known as "versioning," which assured that older versions of the documents were saved and maintained. In addition, check-in and check-out procedures eliminated the possibility of competing revisions and preserved the integrity of the document.

The functionality of search was one of the most notable aspects of SharePoint Portal Server 2000. Its robust search engine indexed content from all around the site, which made it simple for users to access information that was pertinent to their needs in a short amount of time. Users of SharePoint Portal Server 2000 were given the ability to execute keyword searches, refine results based on metadata, and explore related information thanks to improved search algorithms that were made available by SharePoint Portal Server 2000. This helped organizations improve their levels of productivity and knowledge discovery.

One more important feature that was included in SharePoint Portal Server 2000 was the introduction of team sites. Team sites offered devoted locations for groups or departments to successfully interact, share files, and communicate with one another. These websites contained functions such as shared calendars, task lists, and discussion boards, which encouraged frictionless cooperation and made it possible for teams to easily coordinate their operations.

When it came to improving the level of customization and capability offered by SharePoint Portal Server 2000, web components were an extremely important component. Users were able to show content obtained from a variety of sources by incorporating web parts, which were pre-built components that could be added to web pages. For instance, users might integrate notifications, tasks, or document libraries right onto their web sites. This would provide users with convenient access to relevant information and would streamline workflows.

Another area in which SharePoint Portal Server 2000 excelled was in the customization of websites. Users were granted the ability to modify the appearance of their personal portal pages, making them more suitable to their unique requirements and inclinations. They had the ability to add and rearrange web elements, produce individualized views of document libraries, and even establish alerts and notifications to keep themselves informed of recent changes and significant occurrences.

Microsoft Office products have been integrated smoothly into SharePoint Portal Server 2000, which has increased productivity and fostered a more comfortable and familiar user experience. Users were able to save papers directly from within Office apps to document libraries within SharePoint, which not only ensured centralized storage but also made it simple to collaborate on files. This connection expanded to other capabilities of Office, such as the capacity to initiate SharePoint meetings and immediately access SharePoint document libraries from within Outlook.

Following the launch of SharePoint Portal Server 2000, a number of following versions have been distributed; each of these versions builds upon the foundation laid by the version that came before it. The user interfaces, collaboration features, scalability, and interaction with other Microsoft products are some of the areas that have seen significant advancements with these more recent versions. SharePoint Online provides a cloud-based alternative with additional benefits like scalability, accessibility, and frequent updates as part of Microsoft 365 subscriptions, while SharePoint Server 2019, the most recent version as of September 2021, continues to offer advanced capabilities. SharePoint Server 2019 was the most recent version available as of September 2021.

Document Management:

- Users were given the ability to create and manage document libraries with SharePoint Portal Server 2000, which also provided a centralized location for the storage and organizing of data.
- Users were able to monitor changes, evaluate the merits of various versions, and, if necessary, revert to prior iterations thanks to the functionality of versioning.
- Controls for checking in and checking out guaranteed the integrity of the document by preventing conflicting updates from being made.

Search:

- The SharePoint Portal Server 2000 came equipped with a robust search engine that indexed all of the content on the platform.

- This made it possible for users to locate information in a quick and effective manner.
- Using advanced search algorithms made it easier to do keyword searches, use filtering based on metadata, and investigate related content.
- This led to an increase in both productivity and the discovery of new knowledge.

Team Sites:

- Team sites were first offered by SharePoint Portal Server 2000.
- These are dedicated locations that allow teams or departments to communicate and share information with one another.
- The inclusion of tools such as shared calendars, task lists, and discussion boards on team websites encouraged fluid cooperation and made it easier to work as a coordinated unit.

Web Parts:

- SharePoint Portal Server 2000 made use of web parts, which were pre-built components that could be added to web pages in order to improve both their functionality and their level of customization.
- On their own websites, users may incorporate web elements such as notifications, tasks, or document libraries, which would facilitate easy access to relevant content and streamline workflows.

Personalization:

- Users were able to personalize the portal pages they accessed with SharePoint Portal Server 2000, making them more suitable to their unique requirements and preferences.
- Users had the ability to not only add, rearrange, and personalize web elements but also construct individualized perspectives of document libraries and establish alerts and notifications in order to maintain awareness of significant changes and events.

Integrity with Microsoft Office:

- The SharePoint Portal Server 2000 promoted a comfortable and familiar user experience while also improving productivity. This integration with Microsoft Office programs was achieved through seamless integration.
- Users were able to save documents directly from within Office apps to document libraries within SharePoint, which ensured centralized storage and made it easier for users to collaborate.
- Integration was expanded to include additional Office functions, such as the ability to create SharePoint meetings and immediately access SharePoint document libraries from within Outlook.

SharePoint's Continuing Development:

- The beginning of a series of following versions of SharePoint was marked by the release of SharePoint Portal Server 2000.

- Each of these future versions is built upon the foundation that had been established by the version that came before it.
- User interfaces, collaboration features, scalability, and connection with other Microsoft products have all seen significant advancements in more recent versions of the software.

SharePoint Server 2019, which was the most recent version as of September 2021, continued to provide sophisticated features, while SharePoint Online provided a cloud-based alternative with extra benefits and frequent upgrades as part of Microsoft 365 subscriptions. SharePoint Server 2019 was the most recent version. In general, SharePoint Portal Server 2000 included fundamental functionality for document management, collaboration, and search capabilities. This laid the groundwork for the development of SharePoint into a platform that is comprehensive and widely embraced by businesses of all sizes.

SharePoint 2003

In the course of the development of Microsoft's SharePoint platform, the release of SharePoint 2003 in 2003 represented a crucial turning point. Building upon the foundation that was established by its predecessor, SharePoint 2003 provided a number of changes and new features that further improved collaboration, document management, search capabilities, and customization possibilities. These improvements were made possible by the fact that SharePoint 2003 was built upon the platform that its predecessor had established.

Collaboration on documents saw one of the most significant leaps forward in development with SharePoint 2003. It featured capabilities such as document check-in/check-out, version history, and the capability to view and merge changes made by multiple users. Other features included the ability to compare versions of a document. This enabled a number of users to work on the same document simultaneously without compromising the document's integrity and without causing contradictory updates to be made. These characteristics of collaboration enabled teams to work together more efficiently, streamlined document workflows, and ensured that everyone had access to the most recent versions of shared documents.

The functionality of the search engine in SharePoint 2003 was another area that could be improved. The search interface has been improved to make it more user-friendly, and the results of the search now provide improved relevancy as well as choices for filtering. Users were able to do keyword searches inside the documents, file properties, and other content that was saved in SharePoint, which facilitated the users' ability to locate information in a timely and effective manner. The better search capabilities were a significant contributor to the increased productivity and finding of previously hidden knowledge within organizations.

A Web Part structure that was both more powerful and more versatile was introduced in SharePoint 2003. On their SharePoint sites, users were able to construct and customize a variety of components by using Web Parts. Some examples of these components include announcements, calendars, and document libraries. The improved Web Part framework allowed for greater freedom in the creation and personalizing of SharePoint sites in accordance with the particular requirements of each business. Users had the opportunity to quickly add, remove, and configure web parts in order to personalize their SharePoint experiences and enhance the usefulness of the platform.

Microsoft first introduced the concept of user-profiles and the "My Site" feature with the release of SharePoint 2003. User profiles made it possible for users to establish customized profiles that included information about themselves, such as their contact information, interests, and abilities. Every user had access to their own personal site through the "My Site" feature, where they could manage their online profile, documents, and other information. This feature improved the level of personalization and collaboration within the SharePoint environment, making it possible for users to interact with their coworkers, share their expertise, and access the personalized material they had created.

Integration with the various programs that come along with Microsoft Office was enhanced even more in SharePoint 2003. It was possible for users to open and save documents straight from Office apps to SharePoint document libraries. This made it easier for users to work together on files and promoted seamless integration between the two platforms. This integration allowed for effective document management reduced the amount of work that needed to be done twice, and assured that users could work with tools that were already familiar to them.

SharePoint 2003 additionally provides improved tools for managing permissions and security settings. The level of control that administrators have over the process of assigning rights at various levels within the SharePoint environment has become more granular. As a result of the implementation of fine-grained permissions, improved control over access to particular documents, websites, or site regions was made possible. This improved control ensured that sensitive material was safeguarded and that only authorized people could view it.

In addition to this, basic features for business intelligence were introduced in SharePoint 2003. In order to facilitate improved decision-making, data analysis, and data visualization, users were given the ability to generate Excel-based reports and charts and display them directly within SharePoint sites. Because of this capability, businesses were given the ability to successfully exploit their data, obtain insights, and make decisions that were guided by those insights.

SharePoint 2003 brought enhancements over its predecessor, both in terms of its ability to scale and its level of performance. It was built to handle larger amounts of data and support more concurrent users, which ensured that organizations could efficiently manage their rising information needs and accommodate increased user demands. Additionally, it supported more concurrent users.

In terms of capability, convenience, and the variety of customization choices available, SharePoint 2003 represented a huge step forward. It offered businesses a platform that was more powerful and abundant in features, making it suitable for collaboration, document management, search, individualization, and business intelligence. These developments established the framework for further innovations in succeeding versions of SharePoint, allowing it to continue to evolve and meet the evolving demands of organizations all around the world.

Improved Content Review and Approval

In SharePoint 2003, new and improved content approval tools were added, making it possible for businesses to design workflows for content review. This guaranteed that the information went through an evaluation procedure before it was published, thereby preserving quality control and ensuring conformity with the requirements of the organization.

Box for Quick Searches

The Quick Search Box was first introduced in SharePoint 2003, and it serves as a user-friendly and easily navigable search interface for SharePoint websites. Users were able to submit their search queries quickly and acquire appropriate results without having to navigate to a separate page dedicated to the search function. This improved the overall search experience and increased the level of efficiency.

Customizable Site Templates:

With the release of SharePoint 2003, users now have access to a wider variety of customizable site templates. These templates offered pre-configured site architectures for particular business scenarios, such as document management, team collaboration, and project management, and they were available to users as downloadable files. Users could select an appropriate template that met their needs and then modify it in order to make it conform to their particular specifications, hence reducing the amount of time and effort required to create a website.

Warnings and Communications:

New and improved alerting and notification functions were introduced with SharePoint 2003. Users had the ability to set up alerts on certain documents, lists, or libraries, and they would be notified by email whenever there was a change. Because of this, users were able to remain informed about modifications, which made timely collaboration possible and allowed them to keep track of critical changes.

Bin for Recycling:

The Recycle Bin function was first introduced in SharePoint 2003, and it gives users the ability to restore lost items, documents, or sites. It served as a safety net, protecting users from losing data inadvertently and providing them with the possibility to restore content that had been removed in error.

Workspace Documentation Locations:

SharePoint 2003 introduced Document Workspace sites, which offered a dedicated collaboration space for particular documents or projects. These sites could be accessed through SharePoint Online. These websites made it easier for members of a team to work together by providing functions such as shared document libraries, debates, tasks, and events that were unique to the particular document or project at hand.

Integration with a Single Sign-On:

Users were able to access SharePoint sites and resources using their already established credentials thanks to the integration of SharePoint 2003 with the Single Sign-On (SSO) service offered by Microsoft. This integration made the authentication processes more streamlined, enhanced the level of security, and it gave users a more seamless experience while accessing SharePoint.

Improved Views of the Data:

Improved data views were available in SharePoint 2003, and users were given the ability to construct their own unique views of lists and libraries based on a variety of criteria. Users had the opportunity to apply filters, sort columns, and define custom formatting to show data in a manner that was tailored to meet their specific requirements. This resulted in an improvement in both the data visualization and the usability of the system.

Administration That Is Centralised:

The centralized administration capabilities that were introduced in SharePoint 2003 provide administrators with a complete interface for managing SharePoint sites, users, permissions, and settings. These features were introduced in SharePoint 2003. The management and maintenance of SharePoint environments were made easier by centralized administration, which also ensured that the platform maintained uniform configurations and levels of security throughout.

Reporting on the Site's Usage:

SharePoint 2003 included tools for reporting on site utilization, which provided managers with information about user activity, site usage statistics, and content that was most frequently accessed. These reports assisted administrators in understanding user behavior, locating places with high interaction, and making decisions guided by statistics for the optimization of the website and the content strategy.

Integrated support for Active Directory:

SharePoint 2003 was designed to be fully compatible with Microsoft Active Directory, making it possible for businesses to make use of their pre-existing user accounts and security groups for the purpose of managing users and controlling access to SharePoint. This connection streamlined the process of user provisioning and authentication, which ensured that users' experiences were consistent across all of the different platforms.

Increased Capacity to Scale:

The scalability of SharePoint 2003 was improved, enabling organizations to handle larger installations and support expanding data and user volumes. These capabilities were introduced in SharePoint 2003. Because of this, SharePoint was able to adapt to meet the ever-changing requirements of organizations of all sizes, from individual workgroups to multinational corporations.

SharePoint 2007

SharePoint 2007, commonly referred to as Microsoft Office SharePoint Server 2007 (MOSS 2007), was made available to the public in the year 2006. It was the version that came after SharePoint 2003, and it included a wide variety of brand-new features and enhancements. The following is a list of important information regarding SharePoint 2007:

Improvements Made to the User Interface:

SharePoint 2007 debuted a brand new and significantly redesigned user interface, which has a navigation structure that is easier to understand and increases usability. It had an easily modifiable home page, enhanced menus for site navigation, and an intuitive ribbon layout that made it simple to navigate to different commands and operations.

Enterprise Content Management:

SharePoint 2007 introduced increased enterprise content management capabilities, including document management, records management, and online content management. It improved content organization, collaboration, and compliance by providing capabilities such as document check-in/check-out, versioning, content approval procedures, and metadata management. These functions were available to users.

The automation of business processes:

Workflow features were first introduced in SharePoint 2007, and they are backed by Windows Workflow Foundation (WWF). It gave users the ability to develop and automate business processes through the use of configurable workflows, which in turn gave businesses the ability to streamline and optimize their business procedures.

Business Intelligence:

SharePoint 2007 included a number of enhancements to its business intelligence capabilities, including new dashboards, key performance indicators (KPIs), and data visualization tools. Users were able to construct interactive reports, charts, and scorecards to obtain insights from data because it allowed integration with Microsoft Excel and SQL Server Reporting Services.

Excel Services:

Excel Services were first integrated into SharePoint in 2007, giving users the ability to publish and share Excel workbooks on SharePoint sites. Users were given the ability to see, interact with, and refresh Excel-based data via a web browser, which facilitated both collaboration and access to data.

Services for Forms:

Forms Services were first introduced in SharePoint 2007 and made it possible for users to build and publish electronic forms by utilizing Microsoft Office InfoPath. It made it possible for companies to design their own forms, complete with sophisticated controls, built-in data validation, and seamless connectivity with SharePoint workflows.

Business Data Catalog:

The Business Data Catalog, or BDC, was a feature that was introduced in SharePoint 2007 that gave companies the ability to integrate SharePoint with external business systems. These external business systems include databases, web services, and enterprise applications. It made it easier to integrate data from outside sources into SharePoint sites and gave users the ability to interact with and search for data outside of SharePoint without leaving the SharePoint environment.

Content Types:

With the introduction of content types in SharePoint 2007, businesses were given the ability to design and enforce standard metadata, document templates, and behavior across all of their SharePoint sites and libraries. The usage of content categories made content administration easier, ensuring that it was standardized and making it possible to reuse existing information.

The customization options with My Sites:

My Sites was one of the enhanced personalization options available in SharePoint 2007, which was released in 2007. Within the confines of the SharePoint ecosystem, users were given the ability to administer their profiles, documents, tasks, and social connections through the usage of personal site spaces called "My Sites."

Improvements to the Search Engine:

SharePoint 2007 introduced a number of important enhancements to the functioning of the search feature. It pioneered the idea of a search center, which is essentially a centralized location for doing enterprise-wide searches and providing an expanded range of search options, such as contextual searching, search scopes, federated searching, and person searches.

Compatibility with Microsoft Office 2007:

The user experience was consistent and intuitive across both SharePoint 2007 and Microsoft Office 2007, thanks to the deep integration of the two software packages. Users were able to open and save documents straight from Office apps to SharePoint document libraries, which ensured that document management and collaboration went off without a hitch.

SharePoint 2010

Comparing SharePoint 2010 to its predecessor, SharePoint 2007, which was released in 2010, there are a number of new features and additions that were added to SharePoint 2010. The following is a list of important information regarding SharePoint 2010:

Interface with a Ribbon

The ribbon user interface, which was initially introduced in Microsoft Office 2007, was made available in SharePoint 2010 for the first time. The ribbon offered a contextual user interface, which made it simpler for users to access and carry out operations within SharePoint. As a result, navigation and usability were significantly enhanced.

Workspace in SharePoint for

SharePoint Workspace, formerly known as Groove, is a desktop application that was launched in SharePoint 2010. It gave users the ability to synchronize and view SharePoint documents even when they were not connected to the internet. Even when they were not connected to the network, users were able to access and work with SharePoint documents, lists, and library content.

Business Connectivity Services, or BCS, include the following

Business Connectivity Services were first introduced in SharePoint 2010, taking the place of the Business Data Catalog that was present in SharePoint 2007. Directly within SharePoint, users were able to connect and interact with external data sources such as SQL Server databases, web services, and custom applications thanks to BCS's ability to facilitate these connections and interactions.

Solutions Conceived in a Sandbox

Sandboxed solutions were introduced in SharePoint 2010, which enabled a restricted execution environment for custom code. This environment was made available to custom code. Sandboxed solutions allowed companies to deploy and run custom code without affecting the general stability and performance of the SharePoint environment. This was made possible by the isolation provided by the sandbox.

Metadata Management and Tagging

SharePoint 2010 included a number of enhancements to its capabilities for managing metadata. These new features included managed metadata services and term stores. It made it possible for companies to create and enforce standard metadata across all of their sites and libraries, which greatly improved the content's capacity to be organized and found through search. In addition, SharePoint 2010 added a feature known as social tagging, which gives users the opportunity to tag and organize material using keywords in order to make it more discoverable.

Enhanced Experience When Searching

The search experience in SharePoint 2010 was upgraded to be both more powerful and more customized. It contained components like search refiners, contextual search, enhanced person search, visual search, and a search center template enabling the construction of search-driven websites.

Web Content Management

Web content management (also known as WCM) in SharePoint 2010 saw considerable advancements thanks to new features. It provided increased authoring and publishing capabilities, heightened page editing and personalization possibilities, and integration with Microsoft Expression online for more sophisticated online design.

Integration of Microsoft Office Web Apps

Users are now able to read and edit Microsoft Office documents (Word, Excel, PowerPoint, and OneNote) from within their web browsers, thanks to the integration of SharePoint 2010 with Office Web Apps. This feature improved the accessibility of documents as well as the ability to collaborate across a variety of devices and operating systems.

Connecting with Others on Social Networks and Working Together

My Sites, Social Tagging, Activity Feeds, and Expertise Search are just some of the new social features that were included in SharePoint 2010. Better communication and a stronger feeling of community were two of the benefits that resulted from its promotion of social networking, collaboration, and the exchange of knowledge within organizations.

Enhancements to Both Its Performance and Its Scalability

With the speed and scalability enhancements introduced by SharePoint 2010, businesses were better able to manage larger deployments, higher data volumes, and rising user expectations. It ensured efficient and stable operation by introducing features like content caching, request management, and better database performance.

SharePoint 2013

Indeed, SharePoint 2013 was made available to users in the year 2012. It was an enhancement over its predecessor, SharePoint 2010, in many ways, including the addition of new functionality. The following is a list of important information regarding SharePoint 2013:

Responsive Design:

The features of the responsive design were introduced in SharePoint 2013, making it possible for SharePoint sites to dynamically adjust themselves to multiple screen sizes and devices. This enhanced the user experience on mobile devices, making it easier for users to view and interact with SharePoint content using their smartphones and tablets.

App Model:

The new app architecture was introduced in SharePoint 2013, and it offered a strategy to extend SharePoint's functionality that was more adaptable and less dependent on shared resources. Apps in SharePoint 2013 were self-contained components that could be installed, upgraded, and managed individually. This made it possible to customize and integrate third-party apps in a simpler manner.

Microsoft's SharePoint Store:

The SharePoint Store was first introduced in SharePoint 2013, and it is an online marketplace where users can explore, purchase, and download both free and premium SharePoint applications. The SharePoint Store made the process of locating and purchasing apps developed by third-party developers much easier, hence increasing the capabilities and options available for SharePoint deployments.

eDiscovery:

Enhanced eDiscovery functionalities were introduced in SharePoint 2013, giving businesses the ability to locate, store, and process content that is pertinent to meeting legal and compliance requirements. It provided tools for conserving, searching, and exporting content, which assisted companies in more successfully meeting their legal requirements.

Enhanced Capabilities in Social Aspects:

The social capabilities that were first offered in SharePoint 2010 were upgraded in SharePoint 2013. It did so by presenting the Community Site template, which enabled groups to set up discussion boards, so fostering social contacts and community engagement. Additionally, microblogging capabilities and improved social feeds were included in SharePoint 2013 to facilitate improved communication and the exchange of information.

Workflows:

The workflow engine in SharePoint 2013 was completely overhauled, making it simpler to construct and administer workflows. Improvements such as the ability to construct workflows using Microsoft Visio, support for stages and loops in workflows, and closer connection with the workflow capabilities of Office 365 were a few of the new features that were included.

OneDrive for Business, formerly known as SkyDrive Pro:

SkyDrive Pro is a personal document library that was introduced with SharePoint 2013 to provide individual users with a place to store, sync, and share their work documents. SkyDrive Pro gave customers the ability to access their files from a variety of devices and to collaborate with other users in a more streamlined manner. Take note that SkyDrive Pro was eventually rebranded as OneDrive for Business after some time had passed.

Web Component for Content Search:

The Content Search Web Part was a new feature that was introduced in SharePoint 2013, and it made it possible to aggregate and display search-driven content in a manner that was both more flexible and more powerful. It improved both the discoverability of content and the display of that content by allowing users to generate dynamic content rollups from numerous sources that were driven by search and could be customized.

Enterprise Search:

The SharePoint 2013 release introduced a number of important enhancements to the overall corporate search experience. A new search architecture was implemented, which improved both the scalability and performance of the system. The search experience in SharePoint 2013 was also improved, with new capabilities like query suggestions, improved relevancy, and result previews.

App Catalog:

The App Catalog was a new feature that was introduced in SharePoint 2013, and it provided a centralized area for administrators to organize and deploy bespoke apps throughout their organization. Through the use of the App Catalog, administrators were given the opportunity to regulate the availability of apps as well as their deployment, so assuring governance and compliance.

SharePoint 2016

SharePoint 2016, which was published in 2016, brought various new features and enhancements to the table in comparison to SharePoint 2013, which was released in 2013. The following is a list of important information regarding SharePoint 2016:

Hybrid Capabilities:

SharePoint 2016 placed emphasis on hybrid capabilities, making it possible for businesses to link SharePoint deployments hosted on-premises with SharePoint Online hosted in Office 365. This interface made it possible for on-premises and cloud settings to collaborate and synchronize their data in a way that was completely seamless.

Enhancements Made to the User Experience:

SharePoint 2016 placed a primary emphasis on boosting the user experience by delivering a more contemporary and user-friendly interface that was modeled after the way that users interact with Office 365. This was accomplished by enhancing the touch interface, optimizing performance, and improving overall responsiveness. This update improved the user experience of SharePoint and brought it more in line with the rest of the Microsoft ecosystem.

Data Loss Prevention (often abbreviated as DLP):

With the introduction of built-in Data Loss Prevention features in SharePoint 2016, businesses now have the ability to develop and enforce policies designed to prevent the illegal sharing of sensitive information. It is possible to create DLP policies so that they can identify and safeguard sensitive content, so assuring both data security and compliance.

MinRole:

In SharePoint 2016, a new server role design known as MinRole was introduced. This architecture helped simplify farm topologies while also improving performance. Administrators were given the power, by means of MinRole, to delegate particular server roles, such as Front-End, Application, and Distributed Cache, to particular servers. This resulted in more reliable service and more efficient use of available resources.

Large File Support:

With the increase in the maximum file size limit brought about by SharePoint 2016, businesses are now able to store and manage files of a greater size within SharePoint document libraries. This upgrade improves the possibilities of document management for businesses that deal with huge media files or other content categories that require higher storage capacity.

Increased Accuracy in Reporting and Compliance:

Compliance and reporting functions in SharePoint 2016 received upgrades thanks to SharePoint 2016. As a result of the inclusion of capabilities such as document deletion and in-place hold, it enabled businesses to keep and manage content in accordance with regulatory requirements. Additionally, SharePoint 2016 added a brand new compliance center, which can be used to manage compliance regulations and auditing.

Patching with Absolutely No Downtime:

SharePoint 2016 debuted a brand new patching approach, which enabled completely uninterrupted installation of cumulative updates without requiring any downtime. This made it possible for enterprises to implement upgrades and security fixes without disrupting the availability of SharePoint or user access.

Performance Enhancements as well as Scalability:

With the performance and scalability improvements that were introduced in SharePoint 2016, businesses were able to manage larger content databases and a greater number of users. Enhancements such as streamlined website rendering, improved resource management, and faster search indexing efficiency were among the new features that were offered.

Rapid Construction of Site Collections:

With the introduction of faster site collection creation in SharePoint 2016, the amount of time needed to provide new sites was significantly reduced. When establishing new projects, team collaboration spaces, or departmental sites, this enhancement enabled enterprises to rapidly develop new sites while simultaneously increasing their level of productivity.

An improved version of the hybrid search:

Users are now able to search for material across on-premises and cloud environments thanks to enhancements made to hybrid search capabilities in SharePoint 2016, which were released in 2016. It offered unified search results, making it possible for users to access content stored in SharePoint Online as well as on-premises SharePoint 2016 installations through a single search experience.

SharePoint Online and SharePoint 2019

SharePoint Online and SharePoint 2019 are two major updates to SharePoint that Microsoft launched this year. Here are the main differences between the two versions:

As a feature of Microsoft 365, SharePoint Online:

Organizations may now access SharePoint sites and content from any web browser thanks to SharePoint Online, the cloud-based version of SharePoint. It's a tool for working together and getting things done, and it's included in the Microsoft 365 package (formerly known as Office 365).

Constantly Updating:

SharePoint Online, being a cloud service, is always being improved and expanded upon by Microsoft. In this way, businesses can take advantage of new features and upgrades without having to worry about maintaining and deploying updates themselves.

Microsoft 365 integration:

Microsoft Teams, Outlook, and OneDrive for Business are just some of the additional Microsoft 365 apps that work seamlessly with SharePoint Online. By combining multiple resources into one, we may increase efficiency and effectiveness in our teamwork and collaboration.

Storage Space with a Lot of Leeway:

SharePoint Online gives businesses plenty of space to store their data, with storage that can be expanded as needed. SharePoint Online site collections, Microsoft OneDrive for Business, and Microsoft Teams are just some of the numerous storage options available.

Mobility of Access:

SharePoint Online was created to be used on a wide range of mobile devices. SharePoint material is accessible via mobile apps and responsive web design, allowing people to work together from anywhere at any time.

Microsoft SharePoint 2019:

In-Place Coordination:

SharePoint 2019 is the on-premises edition of SharePoint, designed for in-house deployment and administration. SharePoint on Premises is an on-premises version of SharePoint that offers the same capabilities and features as SharePoint Online.

UX in the 21st Century:

SharePoint Online was a major inspiration for SharePoint 2019, which resulted in a more sleek and user-friendly interface. Navigation, responsiveness, and overall usability have all been enhanced thanks to the revamped user experience.

The Power of Hybrids:

The hybrid capabilities that permit a connection between on-premises SharePoint installations and SharePoint Online have continued to be a focal point in SharePoint 2019. Because of this, businesses might take advantage of SharePoint Online for external collaboration while still storing sensitive information in-house.

Efficiency and scalability enhancements:

Organizations can now manage bigger data volumes, and user loads thanks to SharePoint 2019's enhanced performance and scalability. There were enhancements, including streamlined website loading and faster page creation times.

Compliance and Security Improvements:

SharePoint 2019 includes numerous advances to security and compliance. Data loss prevention (DLP) and heightened encryption and security measures were among the features incorporated. The purpose of these changes was to make it easier for businesses to adhere to various security and compliance standards.

Recent Progress in Framework Design:

Support for current development frameworks like SharePoint Framework (SPFx) has been added to SharePoint 2019, enabling the creation of custom solutions and applications via up-to-date web technologies.

Integration with InfoPath and SharePoint Designer:

SharePoint 2019 maintained compatibility with SharePoint Designer and InfoPath, which is important for businesses that use these programs to tailor SharePoint and automate business processes.

SharePoint Online 2020

SharePoint Online, Microsoft's cloud-based version of SharePoint, received a number of fixes and new features in 2020. Some of the most notable features of SharePoint Online in 2020 are as follows:

Lists from Microsoft:

Microsoft Lists is a new software for SharePoint Online that lets users build, manage, and collaborate on lists for keeping tabs on data and procedures. Microsoft Lists allowed for more efficient data management and work flow through the use of adaptable templates, rules, and views.

Sites of Personal SharePoint:

With the introduction of Home Sites in SharePoint Online, a single SharePoint site might serve as the default portal for an entire business. User-tailored and interactive, Home Sites served as a one-stop shop for all the latest updates and announcements.

Syntex for SharePoint

In 2020, Microsoft released a new service called SharePoint Syntex, which was fueled by Project Cortex. Content in SharePoint was automatically categorized and organized using AI and machine learning. SharePoint Syntex was able to extract relevant data from documents and organize it for better searchability and knowledge management.

Cataloging and Library Development:

SharePoint Online's list and library features have been improved with new releases. Column formatting was enhanced, document libraries may have their own unique templates made, and the ability to request files was included so that working with external users would be less of a hassle.

Sites in SharePoint:

With the introduction of SharePoint Spaces in SharePoint Online, businesses are now able to develop and distribute mixed-reality applications that incorporate 3D models, photos, and videos. Users were able to create SharePoint Spaces for a wide variety of purposes, including but not limited to teaching, showcasing products, and giving interactive presentations.

Upgrades to Key Locations:

The Hub Sites feature in SharePoint Online has been upgraded to make it easier to manage and navigate across connected sites. In addition to these enhancements, Hub Sites now have the option to have their designs and branding associated with certain audiences and enhanced navigation.

Upgrades to the Website's Current Design:

SharePoint Online has continued to improve the modern site design experience, with more options for tailoring SharePoint site creation and branding. The option to retrofit existing sites with current layouts and features like configurable site headers was added to the list of enhancements.

Improved Capabilities for Searching:

The search capabilities of SharePoint Online have been enhanced to allow for simultaneous searches across various SharePoint sites and content sources. The appearance of search results and the availability of filtering options have both been improved as part of these updates.

Improvements in External Sharing:

By introducing improvements to external sharing features, SharePoint Online gives businesses more power and safety in their interactions with external users. The option to restrict external sharing to particular domains, create default sharing settings, and set expiration dates for shared links were all a part of this.

Changes to the SharePoint Mobile App:

In 2020, enhancements were made to the SharePoint mobile app that improved its usability on mobile devices. The ability to personalize the app's home screen was added, and navigation was streamlined, along with mobile access to the latest information and headlines.

SharePoint 2023

SharePoint released a number of upgrades in February 2023 with the intention of improving both the employee experience and the efficiency of collaborating. The following is a list of the most important new features and improvements:

Add-on (GA) for Microsoft SharePoint Advanced Management (SAM) from Syntex by Microsoft:

SharePoint has made the Microsoft SharePoint Advanced Management (SAM) add-on available to the general public in order to combat the problems of sprawl and oversharing. SAM has sophisticated security and content management capabilities, which have been purposefully developed for the purpose of working with a variety of documents, including proposals, contracts, invoices, and more. It offers features such as conditional access policies for SharePoint sites and OneDrives, advanced access policies for secure content collaboration, data access governance (DAG) insights for SharePoint sites, limited access control (RAC) policies for SharePoint sites and OneDrives, and more.

The Rebranding of Yammer as Viva Engage

Yammer will now be known as Viva Engage after Microsoft announced the rebranding, which is intended to provide users with a more uniform and enjoyable experience. This rebranding initiative is scheduled to take place over the year 2023 and will include all existing Yammer surfaces. These surfaces include the web, mobile, and integrations like Embed, SharePoint, and Outlook. The upgrade will bring about modifications to the name as well as the logo and icon of the application, bringing it in line with the Microsoft Viva suite.

Viva Engage, formerly known as Yammer, is now integrated with Viva Topics:

Viva Engage's integration with Viva Topics makes it easier for employees of an organization to share their knowledge and find it when they need it. When a user hovers over a topic that has been highlighted in Engage, topic cards can now be displayed thanks to this integration. Additionally, it makes it possible for topic pages and cards to incorporate content from Engage, such as questions, responses, and conversations originating from the applicable community.

Playlists from Microsoft Stream are now available on SharePoint:

Users now have the option to create playlists for video and music files in Microsoft Stream, watch those playlists, and share them with other users. The ability to easily organize media files, share them, and play them back is afforded by this capability. Creators of playlists can invite others to view their playlists, and viewers have the option of viewing or listening to the files in the playlist in the order they were added or skipping between items. The playlists provide access to the full functionality of the player, including chapters, closed captions, and a variety of playing rates.

Updates to OneDrive's Home Screen and Shared Experience:

Updates have been made to OneDrive in order to enhance the overall user experience. Users are now able to prioritize their work more effectively thanks to new features added to the OneDrive Home landing page. These new features include rapid access to frequently used files as well as relevant file activity. The experience of Shared with you has also been improved, making it simpler for users to access content that has been shared from a variety of different sources. These sources include chats, meetings, and emails.

External File Requests in SharePoint Document Libraries:

Document libraries in SharePoint now have access to the functionality that was previously only accessible in OneDrive, which allowed users to make file requests to and receive downloads from third parties. Users have the ability to generate a one-of-a-kind share link that is encrypted and to assign a folder in a SharePoint Document Library as the location where other users can contribute data. The only thing that recipients can do is upload files; they cannot view, edit, remove, or download any of the already existing files, nor can they examine the files that other participants have uploaded.

Power BI can import Microsoft Lists that have been exported as Datasets.

Under the Export menu for Microsoft Lists, a brand new option with the name "Export to Power BI" has been added. In the Power BI service, users may now create datasets that are based on their lists, which makes it easier for users to generate reports and visualize data. This feature provides more possibilities for inline reporting with Power BI in Lists, giving users more leeway to be creative with their data analysis.

Notifications via email on updates to the Rules are now available for Lists and Libraries:

SharePoint modified the rules and email notifications in order to improve the platform's security. In the past, notifications were dispatched from a default email account associated with SharePoint. Notifications will now be delivered from the user's email account that was used to make the most recent change to the rule. By making this adjustment, email notifications will now be more secure and easier to track, and they will be associated with the individual who originally specified or amended the rule.

These upgrades underscore SharePoint's dedication to equipping enterprises with enhanced capabilities for security, collaboration, and document management while still giving users an experience that is straightforward and can be tailored.

BENEFITS OF USING SHAREPOINT

Enhanced Collaboration

Collaboration is made easier thanks to SharePoint, which is one of the most important advantages offered by this platform. SharePoint brings order out of chaos by offering a centralized location from which members of a team can view, share, and modify documents. This reduces the number of different files and versions. This advantage is available to both in-office teams and remote workers, which makes the process of collaboration straightforward regardless of the location of the parties involved.

Efficient Document Management

Businesses now have a more effective tool for managing their papers thanks to SharePoint. It has advanced search facilities, version control, an audit trail, the ability to co-author documents, and more. These are some of the strong document management features that it offers. Not only do these features promote productivity, but they also improve the overall quality of the job by lowering the number of errors and inconsistencies that occur.

Customizable and Scalable

Another significant advantage is the fact that SharePoint may be customized. The platform is highly customizable, allowing businesses to satisfy their particular requirements through the development of one-of-a-kind workflows, forms, and templates. In addition, SharePoint can readily scale to support growing user loads and data quantities as a company expands, which is a significant advantage.

Integrates with Microsoft Ecosystem

Due to the fact that SharePoint is a product developed by Microsoft, it interfaces very well with other software programs developed by Microsoft, such as Word, Excel, and PowerPoint, as well as Teams. Through the usage of this integration, users are able to work on documents from within SharePoint, eliminating the need to switch back and forth between several programs, which improves both productivity and the user experience.

Advanced Search Capabilities

Users are able to quickly and effectively find the information they require because of the extensive search features offered by SharePoint. These capabilities go beyond simple keyword searches and offer features such as search refinement, persons search, and enterprise-wide search, in addition to the ability to search for specific keywords. This makes it simpler to find the particular papers or information that one is looking for, which saves time and reduces frustration.

Security and Compliance

When it comes to security, a primary concern for any company, SharePoint does not fall short of expectations in this area. It provides a full range of security capabilities, such as permission settings, data loss prevention, and enhanced threat protection, among other things. In addition, SharePoint comes equipped with robust compliance capabilities, which make it easier for businesses to satisfy a variety of regulatory obligations.

CHAPTER 2

GETTING STARTED WITH SHAREPOINT

M icrosoft's SharePoint is a powerful collaboration platform that enables businesses to construct and manage their own internal websites, document libraries, and team workspaces. This platform was built by Microsoft. This chapter will walk you through the fundamental concepts and procedures involved in getting started with SharePoint. It does not matter if you are brand new to SharePoint or if you already have some experience with it; this chapter will help you either way.

INSTALLING AND SETTING UP SHAREPOINT

How to Select the Appropriate Version of SharePoint

It is essential to choose the version of SharePoint that is most suitable for your organization's needs before beginning the installation procedure. This must be done before any further steps can be taken. Microsoft provides multiple versions, each of which has a unique set of capabilities and a range of deployment choices. Let's explore the available options:

SharePoint Server

This version of SharePoint offers the most extensive collection of functionality and is ideal for businesses that need full control over their SharePoint environment. SharePoint Server can be installed on-premises, giving businesses the ability to control their own infrastructure and tailor their SharePoint implementation to meet their unique requirements.

SharePoint Online

This version of SharePoint is hosted in the cloud and is included as a component of Microsoft 365 (formerly known as Office 365). It provides a variety of capabilities for document management and collaboration. It is an excellent option for companies that prioritize scalability, flexibility, and low maintenance costs in their IT infrastructure. Microsoft takes care of the underlying infrastructure and upgrades with SharePoint Online, ensuring that users have a pleasant and trouble-free experience.

SharePoint Foundation

SharePoint Foundation is a free, limited-feature edition that offers fundamental collaboration and document management capabilities. SharePoint Foundation is available to anyone who wants it. Even though it lacks some of the more complex features that are available in SharePoint Server, it is a useful starting point for enterprises that are either smaller or have more limited financial resources.

Minimum Requirements for Hardware and Software

It is absolutely necessary to satisfy the hardware and software requirements outlined by Microsoft in order to guarantee a trouble-free installation and the highest possible level of performance from SharePoint. Here are some important factors to take into account:

Minimum Requirements for Hardware:

- A sufficient amount of server resources, such as processing power, random access memory, and storage space, in order to deal with SharePoint's demand.
- The infrastructure of the network is equipped to handle the traffic generated by SharePoint.
- In order to guarantee high availability, redundancy, and fault tolerance methods are taken.

Requirements for the Software:

- Operating systems that are supported, including versions of Windows Server that are compatible with the SharePoint edition that has been selected.
- Components of software that are required before proceeding, such as the .NET Framework, SQL Server, and Internet Information Services (IIS).
- Compatibility with any and all other programs and services that might communicate with SharePoint.

Performing the SharePoint Installation

After you have thoroughly researched the version of SharePoint and made certain that both your computer's hardware and software satisfy the prerequisites, you are ready to move forward with the installation. The installation procedure could have some subtle differences based on the version that is selected and the deployment scenario that is used. The following is a high-level overview of the steps involved in the installation:

The Installation of the SharePoint Server:

- You can either obtain the installation disc or download the SharePoint Server installation package from the website maintained by Microsoft.
- Start the installation process for SharePoint Server, and then follow the on-screen instructions.
- Please include details on the location of the installation, the product key, and the type of installation (full or stand-alone).
- Choose the functions and components you would like to install, such as Search, User Profile Service, and Business Connectivity Services.
- Set up the database by configuring its settings, which include the database server and name, the authentication mode, and any other pertinent parameters.
- Upon completion of the installation procedure, it is necessary to check that SharePoint Server was successfully installed.

Configuration of SharePoint Online:

- Create an account for a subscription to Microsoft 365, which should include SharePoint Online.
- You can use an existing site collection within your Microsoft 365 environment to create a new SharePoint site, or you can create a new site from scratch.
- You can personalize the settings of the site by changing things like the name, logo, theme, and permissions.
- Set up extra SharePoint features like document libraries, list views, and navigation, for example.
- To ensure that correct access control is in place, user accounts should be created, and the relevant permissions should be assigned.
- If necessary, you should either migrate or upload any existing content to SharePoint Online.

Adjusting the Settings of SharePoint

After the installation is complete, it is imperative that SharePoint be configured so that it meets the requirements of your firm. Performing this step requires setting up a number of different farm settings and establishing connectivity with other systems. The following are some essential phases in the configuration:

Farm Configuration

It is necessary to configure the farm settings, which include the farm passphrase, the URL of the central administration, and the server roles. It is important to remember the farm passphrase since it is a security feature that ensures additional servers may only be added to the SharePoint farm by authorized administrators. During the process of configuring the farm, you will choose a one-of-a-kind passphrase that will be required whenever further servers are added to the farm.

In addition, you will be tasked with defining the URL for the central administration, which serves as the web-based administrative interface for SharePoint. This URL offers administrators the ability to carry out a variety of administrative duties, including the configuration of service applications, the management of site collections, and the monitoring of farm health.

In addition to this, you will be responsible for assigning server roles inside the farm. Web front-end servers, application servers, and database servers are the three types of SharePoint servers that perform different responsibilities. Web front-end servers are responsible for processing user requests and serving SharePoint web pages. Application servers are used to host and run customized applications and services, while database servers are used to store SharePoint content and configuration databases.

The Configuration of the Service Application

SharePoint service apps offer supplementary features that, when combined, improve the platform's capacities for content management and collaboration. During the service application configuration phase, you will be responsible for setting up and configuring the appropriate service applications in accordance with the requirements imposed by your organization.

Some critical service applications include:

1. Configuring the Search Service Application: Users are able to search for and obtain relevant information from within SharePoint after the Search Service Application has been configured. You will be responsible for defining the search topology, which will include the number of search components as well as the responsibilities that each component plays, such as crawl, index, and query components.

2. User Profile Service Application: The user profile service application is responsible for storing and managing user profiles in SharePoint, in addition to social data. In order to import user profiles from Active Directory or any other user directory sources, you will need to configure the synchronization connection.

3. Managed Metadata Service Application: this gives you the ability to establish and administer a consolidated taxonomy and metadata across all of SharePoint. You will be responsible for configuring term sets, keywords, and several other metadata attributes in order to ensure the consistent classification and retrieval of content.

4. Business Connectivity Services: By configuring the Business Connectivity Services (BCS), SharePoint is able to integrate and interact with external data sources,

including databases and online services. This is made possible through the use of Business Connectivity Services. You will be responsible for configuring security rights for accessing external data, defining external content kinds, and setting up connection settings.

Interconnectivity and Integrative Capabilities

In order to promote frictionless communication and data interchange, SharePoint frequently requires integration with a variety of different systems and services. Establishing connections with the following will be part of the connectivity and integration configuration that you will be performing:

- Active Directory, which enables SharePoint to synchronize user accounts and provide single sign-on authentication. You will build the trust connection with Active Directory and configure the authentication provider.

- Exchange Server: SharePoint is able to provide functionality such as support for incoming and outgoing email, calendar synchronization, and access to SharePoint documents through Outlook by configuring integration with Exchange Server.

- You can setup SharePoint to interface with third-party applications if the software they utilize is already in use at your company. Setting up connectors, custom web parts, or API connections may be required for this step in order to enable data exchange and functionality between SharePoint and the applications in question.

- SharePoint is compatible with a variety of authentication mechanisms, including Windows authentication, forms-based authentication, and claims-based authentication, among others. You are going to configure the authentication settings based on the security requirements that your organization has, and the user authentication demands that they have.
- Email Sending and Receiving: SharePoint users are given the ability to send and receive emails from within the platform's own lists and libraries. In order to make use of this functionality, you will need to configure the receiving and outgoing email settings, including the specifics of the SMTP server.

The Administration of the Site Collection

Within SharePoint, site collections act as containers for individual sites and provide a logical barrier for managing content and security. In addition, site collections are searchable. During the management of the site collection, you will be responsible for a variety of tasks, including the following:

- Construct and administer site collections, which are SharePoint's equivalent of physical containers that hold individual sites.
- You can customize the settings for the site collection, including the quotas, permissions, and features that are turned on at the site collection level.
- It is important to configure the site collection navigation and branding choices in order to provide users with an experience that is uniform across all sites.

Personalization of the product and branding

Personalize the look and feel of SharePoint by applying themes, developing custom master pages, and using logos and other branding components in your customizations.

To enhance SharePoint's capabilities to satisfy certain business requirements, you can develop and deploy bespoke solutions such as web components, workflows, or bespoke site templates.

Monitoring and Optimization of Performance

In order to monitor SharePoint's performance and locate any potential problems, monitoring, and diagnostic tools should be set up.

Caching, content distribution networks, and database maintenance are all examples of performance optimization approaches that should be used in order to guarantee optimal performance.

NAVIGATING THE SHAREPOINT INTERFACE

Navigating the SharePoint interface can be a significant task for new users. However, once you familiarize yourself with its layout and components, it becomes a powerful tool for managing and sharing content within an organization.

When you first log in to SharePoint, you'll land on the SharePoint home page or a specific SharePoint site, depending on your organization's configuration.

SharePoint Home Page

The SharePoint home page provides an overview of the sites, news, and files that are relevant to you. It's organized into the following sections:

1. **Search Box**: Located at the top, the search box allows you to find sites, files, news posts, and people across SharePoint.
2. **Navigation Bar**: The navigation bar includes links to Home, My Sites, My News, and Recycle Bin. You can use these links to navigate between different sections of SharePoint.
3. **Site Cards**: These are visual representations of your sites. Each card displays the site's name, logo, and recent activity.
4. **News**: This section shows the latest news posts from the sites you're following or frequently visiting.

SharePoint Site

When you navigate to a SharePoint site, you'll encounter a number of components:

1. **Site Header**: This includes the site logo, name, and navigation links.
2. **Site Navigation**: This is typically located on the left side (also known as the Quick Launch) or at the top of modern sites. It provides links to important locations on the site, like pages, libraries, and other subsites.

3. **Command Bar**: This bar includes various commands, such as new, upload, sync, etc. The commands change based on the context. For example, if you're in a document library, you'll see options to upload files, create folders, sync to your desktop, and more.

4. **Main Content Area**: This is where your site content lives, such as text, images, documents, lists, and more.

5. **Site Contents**: Available from the site settings, this shows all the libraries, lists, and apps created on the site.

UNDERSTANDING SHAREPOINT SITES AND SITE COLLECTIONS

As you start to unfurl the layers of SharePoint, you'll find these fundamental elements serving as the blueprint for its rich array of features and functionalities.

Let's begin by exploring SharePoint Sites. Essentially, a SharePoint Site is a dedicated workspace meticulously designed to serve a particular team or purpose. Whether it's a project team on the cusp of a breakthrough, a bustling department striving to streamline resources, or an entire organization aiming to share and manage its knowledge, a SharePoint Site is a customizable haven. The true charm of a SharePoint Site is its adaptability - it's malleable and built to meet the unique needs and work styles of diverse teams and individuals.

Every SharePoint Site is equipped with an array of features tailored to foster collaboration and information dissemination. This toolset includes document libraries for storage, lists for efficient data management, team calendars for seamless scheduling, and discussion boards for effortless team communication, among many others. Each Site also offers an assortment of ways to curate and display information - think intuitive navigation menus and tailored web parts.

So, where does a SharePoint Site reside? This brings us to the realm of Site Collections. Simply put, a Site Collection is akin to a big family of interrelated SharePoint Sites. It is a hierarchical assembly of Sites sharing common features such as permissions, content types, and templates. At the apex of this hierarchy rests the root site, donning the role of a parent to all other Sites (or subsites) nestled within the Site Collection.

One of the standout advantages of Site Collections lies in shared administration. As a Site Collection Administrator, you are gifted with the ability to define permissions or features that span across all Sites within the collection. This significantly cuts down the time and effort demanded for managing each site individually. Further sweetening the deal, Site Collections enable sharing of content types, columns, and templates, ensuring uniformity in data management across Sites.

Planning your Site Collections, however, warrants careful consideration. You must mull over several factors - the intended purpose of the Sites, the expected number of users, the volume of data, security mandates, and the necessity for distinct policies or settings. Your aim should be to strike a balance, ensuring administrative ease without compromising on the flexibility for Sites to cater to their unique requirements.

Remember, the structure you adopt holds the power to impact not just the user experience but also the performance of the system and the integrity of your data. Thus, grasping the concepts of SharePoint Sites and Site Collections isn't just about understanding their definitions; it's about comprehending how they can be effectively structured to bolster your specific needs.

How to Create SharePoint Site

Creating a SharePoint Site is a simple and intuitive process, but it does require the necessary permissions. Here's a step-by-step guide to help you:

1. **Sign in to SharePoint:** First, you need to sign in to your Office 365 or Microsoft 365 account. Once logged in, navigate to the SharePoint section of your Microsoft 365 homepage.

2. **Create a new site:** On your SharePoint homepage, you'll find a "+ Create site" button, typically located in the top left corner of the page. Click on this button to start the process of creating a new SharePoint site.

3. **Choose your site type:** SharePoint provides two types of sites: Team Site and Communication Site.
   - A **Team Site** is ideal when you want a site where team members or colleagues can collaborate, share documents, and communicate. This type of site is often linked with an Office 365 group, which provides additional features like a shared mailbox or a shared calendar.

- A **Communication Site** is perfect when you want to share information broadly, such as company news, reports, or status updates, with a large audience.

Choose the type of site that best fits your needs.

4. **Configure your site:** Next, you'll be prompted to provide some information about your new site:

   - **Site Name:** Give your site a name. This name will appear in the site URL, the site header, and in the site navigation.

   - **Site Description:** Provide a brief description of the purpose of the site. This will help other users understand what the site is for.

   - **Site Design:** Select a design that suits the purpose of your site. You can choose from Topic, Showcase, and Blank for Communication Sites, or you can simply choose the default for Team Sites.

   - **Site Owners and Members:** Specify the owners and members of your site. Site owners have full control over the site. Site members, on the other hand, have fewer permissions but can typically add and edit content.

5. **Create your site:** Once you've configured your site, click on the "Finish" or "Create" button to create your site. SharePoint will then set up your new site, which may take a few moments.

6. **Customize your site:** After the creation process, you'll be taken to the new SharePoint site. Here, you can start customizing your site by adding pages, lists, libraries, and web parts according to your needs. Remember, the appearance and structure of your SharePoint site can be changed at any time, so don't worry about getting it perfect from the start.

CHAPTER 3

UNPACKING SHAREPOINT LISTS AND LIBRARIES

SHAREPOINT LISTS AND LIBRARIES

SharePoint Lists and Libraries, two essential elements of the SharePoint platform, make it possible to store information, organize that information, and collaborate on its management.

SharePoint Lists

SharePoint Lists are organized with rows and columns for data storage, just like tables in Microsoft Excel. Attachments, such as photographs or written materials, can be added to lists in addition to the other types of content. There are many different types of lists, including calendars, to-do lists, contact lists, announcement lists, link lists, discussion boards, and survey forms. These lists may be shared with coworkers, teams, and anyone with access to them. Lists in SharePoint can be organized in a dynamic and flexible manner, and they can be constructed either from scratch or by using pre-made templates. Once the lists have been created, you can include columns, construct views, sort, arrange, format, and filter the lists to convey critical information effectively. In addition, automation can be utilized to increase productivity and decrease wait times. The new lists feature in SharePoint, which offers a responsive and mobile-friendly user experience, has made engaging in direct collaboration from a team site feasible. This was made possible by the SharePoint team.

Step 1: Log in to your SharePoint site.

Our journey begins by logging into your SharePoint site. Easy enough, right? Launch your preferred web browser, be it Chrome, Firefox, or even Edge, and key in the URL for your SharePoint site. If your site requires credentials (and most do), a prompt will appear asking you to enter your username and password. With the correct details in hand, key them in, and voila! You're in.

Step 2: Navigate to your desired SharePoint list.

Next up, we'll need to find the list you're yearning to open. Now, if this is a list you've been working with regularly or have marked as a favorite, it may conveniently appear on the left-hand navigation menu. This is known in SharePoint lingo as the Quick Launch Bar." Simply click on the name of the list to open it.

If, however, your list is playing hide and seek and is not visible on the Quick Launch bar, worry not. SharePoint has you covered. Head to the site's settings menu, usually located in the top-right corner of your screen (look for the gear icon). From the dropdown options, click on 'Site Contents.' This will open a new page showing all the lists, libraries, and other apps that your SharePoint site houses. Scroll through until you find the list you're seeking, then click on it to open.

SharePoint Libraries

SharePoint Libraries, or Document Libraries, are specialized lists that may be established in SharePoint to store, create, organize, and manage a wide variety of documents and files. These SharePoint Libraries are also referred to as Document Libraries. Because of these libraries, team members can share files with one another and retain metadata, both of which make it simpler to locate and recognize files for subsequent use. Every SharePoint library has a list of files and pertinent information about those files, such as the date and time of the most recent update and the person who made the Edit. Documents created in Microsoft Office Word, spreadsheets created in Microsoft Excel, presentations created in Microsoft PowerPoint, photographs, and other files can all be saved in a SharePoint library.

How to Excess

1. Firstly, open your preferred web browser and navigate to the URL of your SharePoint site. You may need to enter your username and password if prompted.
2. Once you're inside your SharePoint site, you'll find a navigation pane on the left side of your screen. This is

called the Quick Launch bar. If the library you wish to access is listed there, simply click on its name. If it's not there, don't worry; just head to the next step.

3. In case your library isn't in the Quick Launch bar, go to the 'Site Contents' page. You can find this by clicking on the gear icon (usually located at the top-right corner of the screen), then selecting 'Site Contents' from the dropdown menu.

4. The 'Site Contents' page will show all the lists, libraries, and other components available on your SharePoint site. Here, finds the library you're interested in and click on it.

CREATING AND MANAGING LISTS

- Select the "Lists" tab in the left navigation pane.

- When you access SharePoint, you may notice this tab on the left side of the webpage where it is located. It incorporates all preceding lists and acts as the basis for any new lists you may construct in the future.

- From the menu, select the "New" option. (The "List" option is one of the dropdown menu options displayed when you click this button, which is located quite close to the top of the list area.)

- Select the "List" option.

- By selecting this option from the dropdown menu, you will be able to open a new dialogue box in which you can create a new list.

- Give the list a name for easy reference. (The headline of the list should be a brief and perceptive sentence that encapsulates the list's purpose.)
- If you so like, you can include a description. (This more detailed explanation can help readers comprehend the function of the list when they examine it by providing them with additional information about the list itself.)
- Choose the type of list you want to make. (Depending on the circumstances, the list may be able to include different kinds of things. Calendar, contact management, and task management are just some available options.)

CUSTOMIZING LIST COLUMNS AND VIEWS

Customizing Columns

- To modify the columns in a SharePoint list, follow the methods provided here.
- To get started, launch the list that needs to be modified.
- Select the "Add column" button, which can be found on the right side of the screen next to the columns that are presently being used.
- Determine the type of column that will be included in the table (for example, a single line of text, a number, a choice, etc.).
- After making any other settings that may be required, type the name of the column you are editing.
- Select the "Save" option to commit the changes you've made.

Add Items

To initiate the creation of a list in SharePoint, select the "Items" tab in the window to the left of the navigation bar. When you perform this action, the page that allows you to view things that have previously been generated as well as add new ones will be opened. Click the "New Item" button on the toolbar to add a new item. You will then be led to a page where you can provide the required information in each column. The columns will be formatted differently according to the type of list that you are making. After entering all the necessary information, select the "Save" button using the dropdown menu. After your newly generated item has been saved, you can view it on the "Items" tab for further inspection.

Share the List

To begin creating a list in SharePoint, you must first locate and select the "Share" icon, which is located in the upper right-hand corner of the page. In the subsequent dialogue box that will pop up, you can type in the names of the individuals with whom you want to share your list. After inputting the users' names, you will be given the option to select the permission level for each user. Depending on the permissions granted to them, they may be able to, among other things, alter the list, read it, or remove items from it. After selecting the appropriate permission level for each user, make the modifications by clicking the "Share" option. After that, you can validate the changes by clicking the "OK" button at the bottom of the window. The list has now been shared with the individuals you've chosen, and the amount of permission you've granted them will determine how much access they have to the list.

View the List

1. Follow these steps to generate a view for the list you have stored in SharePoint.
2. 1. The first step is to open the list that needs to change its view.
3. 2. Select "All Items" from the dropdown menu that can be found in the upper left corner of the list (directly above the column headers).
4. 3. Choose "Create new view" from the dropdown menu on the page's bottom.
5. 4. Choose a view type (List, Calendar, or Gallery) and configure the parameters you want to use, such as filters, sorting, and the columns displayed in the view.
6. 5. After giving your view a name, click the "Save" button to finalize creating the new view.

UPLOADING AND MANAGING DOCUMENTS IN LIBRARIES

You can easily create new documents in the library through the New menu in SharePoint. You can also upload documents that were created offline.

Follow these procedures to add a document to your document library:

- Go to the library where you want to upload the document by browsing there.
- To enter the file selection dialogue, click Upload and select the Files option.
- When you have located the file you want to upload, click Open.
- You can use this way to upload a library with multiple files or entire folders.
- (Drag and drop functionality is supported by SharePoint as well. When accessing the library, merely drag and drop the files or folders to any location in the browser window. This will have the same effect as steps 2 and 3 below in that SharePoint will upload the files or complete folders and any subfolders containing the contents of these folders to the library.)
- This will start the uploading of files.
- You'll see that SharePoint displays both a preview and file details.
- When you click on the file preview in the right-side pane, the file is activated, and you may examine its whole contents in that pane.
- You must enter data in the necessary fields for this document before it is made publicly available. At this stage, give your file a friendly title. In this document's Properties box, click the Edit All link. If you cannot see

the properties window, make sure the document is chosen.

- Click the Save button after entering or choosing the necessary data for the document.

VERSIONING AND DOCUMENT CONTROL

The following actions need to be taken to activate and set up versioning in a SharePoint Online library:

1. Select the library where you want to activate versioning, then navigate to that location.
2. Navigate to the "Settings" menu, and pick "Library Settings."
3. Navigate to the "Versioning Settings" page within "Library Settings."
4. The "Versioning Settings" tab of a document collection will provide you with a number of different alternatives from which to choose. These are the following:
   - The choice to demand prior content approval for any things that are submitted.
   - The ability to choose to generate a new version of a file whenever an existing file in the document library is modified.
   - The option to produce either major or minor versions, as well as the limit on the total number of versions and draughts that can be kept.

- The ability to select which users are permitted to access draught items.

5. Once you've chosen your desired settings, click "OK."

Repeat the procedures from the previous section and, on the "Versioning Settings" page, pick the option labeled "No versioning" to disable versioning in a SharePoint Online library.

Follow these steps to examine an older version of an item or document stored in a SharePoint Online library and restore or remove that version.

1. In order to view the history of the item or document you are looking for, you must first locate it in the library.
2. Next to the item, look for the three dots (...) and click on them. Then pick "Version History."
3. In the "Version History" dialogue box, move your mouse pointer over the date link and click on the down arrow to see the list of options.
4. The following options will be available to select from when using the menu:
   - View
   - Restore
   - Delete
   - Reject this version (only possible for documents that have already been authorized)
5. Click the "X" in the top right corner of the dialogue box to close it once you have finished the activities it requested of you.

CHAPTER 4

DELVING INTO
SHAREPOINT DOCUMENTS

W hen working with the files in your SharePoint document library, you have several options. These include adding new files, copying existing files, and moving items across folders. The work that you and other people have done on the files may be viewed, and you can save earlier versions of the files so that you have access to them if you need to restore them. You and your team have great control over the files you work with, including where they are stored, what they contain, and how they are accessed.

COLLABORATING ON DOCUMENTS

One of the most critical functions of SharePoint is document collaboration. This function enables several users to work on the same document simultaneously, monitor changes made to the page, and even revert back to earlier versions of the document if necessary. Using SharePoint to collaborate on documents can be done as follows:

- Select the file that you want other people to see.
- Select the Share option.
- Here are the three options available to you:
- Enter the people's names or email addresses and, if you'd like, a message to let them know that you're sharing the paper with them to let them know that you're sharing the paper with them. After you have finished preparing, select the Send button.
- Select the option "Copy Link" to generate an email or instant messaging-compatible link to the file you may use to share the file with others.
- By selecting Outlook, you can visit the online version of Outlook and add a link to the file in a new email message.

CHECKING OUT AND CHECKING IN DOCUMENTS

If you want to make changes to a file stored on a SharePoint site and you want to make sure that no one else can edit it, you will need to check out the file first. After you have checked out the file, you can make changes to it either online or offline, save your changes, and then continue as necessary.

After you have completed making changes and checked the item back into the library, other users can view your adjustments and make their own additions to the file if they have permission to do so. You also have the option to discard your checkout entirely if you change your mind about making or retaining any changes to the file. This will leave the version history unaltered.

Check Out Files

Some library systems are set up to require patrons to check out files. If file checkout is required, you will be prompted to check out any files that you want to change if you choose to do so. After you have finished working with the file, you must either check it back in or erase the checkout.

If you are willing to let other people update the document while you are working on it, then there is no need to check it out of the library if the library does not mandate that you do so.

1. Navigate to the library in which you have saved your document.
2. For example, if you want to visit the Documents library, click the Documents tab first.
3. Make sure you have selected the file (or files) you want to check out.
4. Select Check Out from the menu with three dots that are located above the list of documents.
5. The option to check out a file may be found in the menu that consists of three dots and is located above the file list in the SharePoint Library.

Notes:

1. A little icon shows in the appropriate location when the file is checked out. A file that has been checked out from the library is indicated by a tick mark with a very small red circle surrounding it.
2. If you get this message, the file is checked out to either you or another user. If you move the mouse pointer over the file name while it is highlighted, you can see the name of the user who currently has the file checked out.
3. In the conventional user interface, the Check Out function can be accessed through the Files tab of the ribbon.

Check-in

1. You should check in using the document library on SharePoint.
2. Navigate to the library in which you saved your file; for example, to get to the Documents library, you first need to click the Documents library's name.
3. You must select the file(s) you want to check before continuing.
4. Select Check-in from the menu of three dots above the Documents list.
5. The "Check In" option may be found in the menu that consists of three dots and is located above the file list in the SharePoint Library.
6. Hit the "OK" button. The checkmark disappears from the file icon, and the green arrow moves away from it when the file is checked back in.

DOCUMENT CO-AUTHORING

Co-authoring documents in SharePoint emerges as an indispensable feature for facilitating collaborative tasks. It allows various users to work synchronously on the same document in real-time, vastly boosting team productivity and fostering enhanced cooperation. This section of the chapter will navigate you through the complexities and simplicities of document co-authoring in SharePoint.

Understanding Document Co-Authoring

Before we explore the support SharePoint provides for document co-authoring, it's essential to know what co-authoring entails. At its core, document co-authoring enables two or more individuals to collaborate on a document at a time, eradicating the need for time-consuming sequential edits and associated delays.

SharePoint has stepped up as a powerful platform for document co-authoring, compatible with many file types, encompassing Word documents, PowerPoint presentations, and Excel spreadsheets. Thanks to its flawless integration with Microsoft Office 365 and other related applications, SharePoint offers a vibrant and engaging co-authoring experience.

An Overview of Its Key Features

- Collaboration in real-time: The co-authoring feature of SharePoint enables users to view changes made by others without having to refresh the page. This capacity increases productivity, lowers the likelihood of disagreements, and guarantees that everyone is on the same page (both physically and figuratively).

- Version control: SharePoint automatically keeps track of document versions. If you ever find yourself in a situation where you need to revert to a former state or figure out what modifications were made and by whom, you will find this function to be quite helpful.

- Access control: SharePoint gives you the ability to specify access rights on a wide variety of levels, from the site level all the way down to the document level. You have the ability to decide who may read, modify, or delete files, giving you a granular degree of control and security.

- Comments and notes: Users have the ability to leave comments and notes right in the document. This function makes it easier for members of the team to communicate with one another and provides a means of providing context or explaining changes.

How to Use SharePoint's Co-Authoring Function

Follow the steps below in order to begin working on a document with many authors in SharePoint:

- Uploading the document is the initial stage, and this must be done in order to ensure that the material may be accessed later.

- Share the document: Once the document has been posted, you will have the ability to share it with the members of your team. They will get an offer to modify the document when it is sent to them.
- Start co-authoring: Members of the team can access the document and immediately begin making edits. Every user will be able to see the changes that have been made in real-time, even if they were made by a different user.

Considerations and limitations

Although SharePoint is an excellent platform for document collaboration, there are a few constraints to keep in mind, including the following:

- Conflict resolution: When two people edit the same area at the same time, it's possible that disputes will emerge. SharePoint makes an effort to address issues, but it is not without its limitations.
- File type and size: Co-authoring is not supported by all file formats, and huge files may create performance concerns.
- Latency in the network: The success of real-time cooperation is strongly dependent on the availability of the network. It is possible that changes will not show in real time in situations with low bandwidth.

DOCUMENT METADATA AND PROPERTIES

In SharePoint, the information that is utilized to categorize and categorize content is referred to as "metadata," and the word "metadata" itself comes from the word "metadata." This could take the form of creating specialized metadata fields or document properties. Using metadata in SharePoint makes organizing, locating, and keeping track of information are all made more accessible by using metadata in SharePoint. The following is a synopsis of how SharePoint deals with metadata::

Document Properties:

A few examples of the built-in properties attached to every document in SharePoint include the name of the file, the title, the author, and the last date it was modified. Examining and editing these attributes is possible by choosing the document and selecting "Details" or "Properties" from the document library. This will bring up the appropriate menu.

Custom Columns:

In addition to the document attributes that are already present, you have the option of adding new columns to your document library so that you can save more metadata. You might, for instance, decide to add a column labeled "Project Name" or "Document Status." When you create a custom column, any document in that library will have access to it and be able to utilize it.

Metadata Navigation and Filtering:

You can search for documents in a library using SharePoint's metadata and browse through those documents. For example, if you have a column labeled "Project Name," you can use that column to filter the library so that it only displays papers that are associated with a particular project. In addition, you can organize the papers into groups according to the metadata associated with them, such as the author or the document's status.

Content Types:

A content type is a reusable collection of metadata (columns), workflow, behavior, and other attributes for a specific group of items or documents in a SharePoint list or document library. This collection is also known as a content template. By utilizing content types, you can centralize and repurpose the management of the information and behavior associated with a document or item type.

Term Store:

In addition, you have access to SharePoint's Term Store, a tool that operates as a centralized database for metadata organization. Your SharePoint sites can make use of hierarchies that have been constructed out of the terms you've defined. This helps to ensure that the metadata on various websites and document libraries are consistent.

Metadata in Search:

SharePoint uses metadata to improve the precision and relevancy of search results. When you search for a document in SharePoint, the platform may use metadata to filter and sort the results of the search. In addition, you can search for documents according to the metadata they contain.

Document Metadata and Properties

Using SharePoint to create, use, and manage taxonomies and metadata fields will assist you in organizing and locating the content you have uploaded. The following is a list of the steps:

1. Create Metadata Columns:
2. Items in a SharePoint list or library can have metadata added to them through custom columns, which the user can construct. These columns can store many different types of data, including text, numbers, dates, and options.
3. Please move to the list or library that will have the column added to it and navigate there.
4. On the right side of the ribbon, select the "Add column" option.
5. When selecting the type of column to add, you can add a single line of text, a number of columns, a choice column, etc.
6. Include in the details of the column the column's name, description, and any other attributes relevant to the type of column.
7. Ensure that you click "Save."

Use Content Types:

You can design a content type that includes all of the columns contained in any groupings of columns you frequently use. After that, the content type can be added to any list or library, which will result in adding all of the columns associated with the content type to the given list or library.

1. Navigate to the Site Settings menu.
2. Within the selection of "Web Designer Galleries," select the option labeled "Site content types."
3. Select the "Create" option to initiate the production of a new content type.
4. Choose the content type that will serve as the new content type's parent, then give the new content type a name and a description.

5. After generating the content type, you can add columns to it. When you are completed, you should add the content type to any list or library on your website.

Use the Term Store:

The Term Store, a central repository for managing terms and term sets, can be utilized for more intricate information needs.

1. Navigate to the Site Settings menu.
2. From the "Site Administration" menu, choose the "Term store management" option.
3. The Term Store allows you to construct new term sets, add words to those sets, and regulate the properties of the terms themselves.

Manage Metadata:

After you have set up your metadata fields, check to see that they are being utilized appropriately.

1. Perform routine reviews of your metadata fields to ensure they remain valuable and relevant in your organization.
2. While adding new items or editing existing ones, users should be shown how to use the metadata fields.
3. Keep a log of how your metadata is being used. Are there some fields, for example, that people tend to leave blank most of the time? Exist any fields that the consumers find to be difficult to understand?

Always remember that the key to successful metadata management is to keep things as straightforward as possible while still meeting the requirements of your organization. Users are more likely to need clarification when confronted with excessive complexity, which might result in inconsistent or erroneous metadata.

CHAPTER 5

AUTOMATING WITH SHAREPOINT

Workflows in SharePoint are pre-built small programs that may automate and streamline various business processes. Workflows may involve anything from monitoring the development of a standard technique to collecting signatures, comments, or approvals on a plan or document. This could be done in a variety of different ways.

SharePoint comes with several different workflows that have already been established, and you are free to use any of these workflows without making any further adjustments. You can alter them using tools such as SharePoint Designer or Microsoft Power Automate (formerly known as Microsoft Flow), or you can build a workflow tailored to your own company's procedures using tools such as SharePoint Designer.

CREATING AND MANAGING WORKFLOWS

1. Locate the library for which you want to create the flow.

2. In the command bar, look for Power Automate under the Automate option.

3. Then select Create a Flow.

4. A flow template can be chosen from the right-hand panel. One of the pre-built flows can be used or serve as the basis for a bespoke flow.

5. Connect Power Automate to a list or library on SharePoint.

6. Take to the Power Automate designer, please. You should be able to alter your process once you get here.

   a. Your workflow begins depending on the trigger, which is the initial step in the flow. After the initial action, you can add more. All of these are reliant on the previous action.

   b. One kind of flow occurs when an item is added or altered automatically. A second sort of flow is initiated only after you choose an item.

      i. Click the Automate menu in the SharePoint command bar to begin this flow. Depending on the trigger type you previously chose, the flow may begin automatically or manually from the command bar.

      ii. Be sure to update the template's default values or add any required information. Click Edit after selecting Send Email to change the default values. Changes to the email's appearance and the display of extra fields from the SharePoint item are available for the Send Email action.

7. Click Create Flow after configuring the flow.
8. Click Done once the flow has been constructed.

AUTOMATING BUSINESS PROCESSES WITH POWER AUTOMATE

You may automate business procedures and workflows across various apps and services by using Microsoft's solution called Power Automate (which was initially known as Microsoft Flow). Microsoft offers power Automate. It is possible to automate various business processes within SharePoint Online utilizing this. The following is a brief explanation of how to carry it out:

Make a New Flow in Power Automate

First things first: log in to Power Automate. On the home page, select "Create" from the menu on the left side of the page. You will be presented with various flow options, including Automated, Instant, Scheduled, Desktop, or Business process flow. Make your decision based on what is most beneficial to your organization.

Choose Your Trigger:

Following the selection of the flow type, you will be required to choose a trigger for the flow. The process is started by a series of occurrences known as triggers. The phrases "When an item is created" and "When a file is created (properties only)" are both examples of SharePoint triggers. Other possible triggers include "When a folder is created." After deciding on a trigger, you will need to provide details about your SharePoint site and choose the specific list or library where the trigger event will take place.

Add Steps to Your Flow:

After selecting your trigger, you will have the opportunity to add actions, conditions, or other controls to determine the following steps in your flow. For instance, if you want to send an email whenever a new item is published to SharePoint, you can use Office 365 Outlook to add "Send an email (V2)." This would fulfill your requirement.

Configure the Action:

Depending on the course of action that you decide to take, you might be asked to provide additional information at some point. If you want to send an email using the "Send an email" action, you have to specify the recipient, the topic, and the email body. Utilize the trigger's dynamic content in order to make changes to these fields.

Save and Test Your Flow:

After you have determined the steps, you should save your flow and test it to ensure everything works out as expected. You have the option in Power Automate to either manually carry out the trigger action or use data from previously completed runs to verify your flow.

Monitor Your Flow:

You can monitor the use of your flow and its overall efficiency through the Power Automate website. On the "Activity" page, you will see a summary of all runs, including unsuccessful ones. This will assist you in locating any issues and repairing them.

Steps To Automate Business Processes

Step 1: Log into Power Automate

- Go to the Power Automate website at https://flow.microsoft.com in your web browser.
- Use your Microsoft credentials to log in.

Step 2: Create a new Flow

- Choose "Create" from the left-hand navigation panel on the Power Automate home page.
- Because we want our procedure to be automatically triggered, so choose "Automated cloud flow."

Step 3: Configure your Trigger

- You will be asked to give your flow a name and select a trigger to initiate it.
- In the "Flow name" box, enter a name for your flow.
- Type "SharePoint" in the "Choose your flow's trigger" box and choose "When an item is created" from the dropdown list.

Step 4: Specify SharePoint Site and List

- You'll be prompted to enter information about the particular list and your SharePoint site.
- Choose the URL for your SharePoint site in the "Site Address" box.
- Choose the list where the trigger event will occur in the "List Name" box.

Step 5: Add an Action

- Select "Add an action" after clicking "New Step."
- Enter "email" in the search box, then click "Office 365 Outlook - Send an email (V2)".

Step 6: Configure the Action

- Give specifics about the email. Enter the recipient's email address in the "To" field.
- The "Subject" and "Body" fields should be filled in. You can use your trigger's dynamic content. For instance, you can put the title of the item you generated in SharePoint in the email's subject line or body.
- Click the " Show advanced options " link to add other information, such as importance or attachments, and click the "Show advanced options" link.

Step 7: Save and Test Your Flow

- Click "Save" in the top right corner once the action has been configured.
- You may evaluate your flow by selecting the "Test" button in the upper right corner. You can perform the trigger action manually or use information from earlier runs.

Step 8: Monitor Your Flow

- You can check the performance of your flow after it has been tested and saved by visiting the Power Automate website.

- In the left navigation panel, select the "Activity" tab to view a list of all runs, both successful and unsuccessful.

This is just a simple example to get you started with automating business operations in SharePoint using Power Automate; remember to change these procedures according to your needs.

CHAPTER 6

SAFEGUARDING SHAREPOINT

The default permission levels are established sets of privileges that you can apply to certain individuals, groups of users, or security groups. These default permission levels are decided by the functional requirements of the users and the security concerns. The permission settings for a SharePoint Server site collection are managed at the site collection level, and by default, permissions are inherited from the object's parent.

UNDERSTANDING SHAREPOINT SECURITY CONCEPTS

The functionality of the permissions in SharePoint relies heavily on this feature. This is how Office 365 Group Sites and Communication Sites operate now, and it is quite similar to how SharePoint sites have operated for many years. The concept is very fundamental. Every library has a connection to these three pre-defined security groups by default:

- Site Members
- Site Owners
- Site Visitors

Users who are only allowed to read are visitors to your library. These users can only read and download content from the website.

Site Members are the people you add, edit, and delete. These users can create new content (documents, pages, announcements, and events), edit existing content, delete existing content, view existing content, and download existing content. They also can give stuff to other people.

You have full authority over the site's administrators. These individuals have access to everything that Visitors and Members have access to, in addition to the ability to manage navigation, develop additional library elements, and ensure the site's safety. You are free to design your security groups and add them to the library in order to enable a greater number of groups and specific rights.

MANAGING SHAREPOINT GROUPS AND USERS

You can add or remove SharePoint groups if you're a site owner or site collection administrator. You can use groups to restrict access to your sites and content by determining which people belong to these groups. Because the site collection is the standard root of site permissions, groups are, by default, created at the site collection level. Additionally, you can add users to a SharePoint group you build for a subsite.

Create a group

1. Click Settings, followed by Site Settings, on your personal or team website.
2. Click People and Groups under Users and Permissions on the Site Settings page.
1. Opens the group page.
2. In the left navigation, select Groups.
3. To create a new group, select New on the Groups page.
4. Enter unique owner information for this security group in the Group owner box.
5. Specify who may view and update the membership of this Group in the Group Settings section.
6. Choose the options you want for requests to join or quit the Group in the Membership Requests section. The email address to which requests should be forwarded can be specified.
7. Select a permission level for this Group in the Give Group Permissions to this Site section.
9. Press Create.

Add users to a group.

Users may join groups at any time.

1. Click Share on your personal or team website. 2. The words Invite people to Edit or Invite others are displayed by default in the Share dialogue box that occurs. By doing this, you're inviting the people you've added to the SharePoint Members group. Click Show Choices, then select a different SharePoint group or permission level from the list under Select a group or permission level to select a different group and permission level.

2. Type the name or email address of the user or Group you wish to add in the Enter names, email addresses, or Everyone box. Select the name to add it to the text field when it appears in the confirmation box below your submission.

3. Repeat steps 1 through 3 to add more names.

4. Add a customized message to be sent to the new users in the Send a personalized note along with this invitation.

5. Press Share.

Remove users from a group.

1. Click Settings, followed by Site Settings, on your personal or team website.

2. Click People and Groups under Users and Permissions on the Site Settings page.

3. Click the name of the Group you wish to delete users from in the Quick Launch on the People and Groups page.

4. Click Actions, choose to Remove members from Group, and then check the boxes next to the members you wish to delete.

5. Select OK in the confirmation window.

Grant site access to a group

1. Click Settings, followed by Site Settings, on the Team Site.

2. Click Site Permissions under Users and Permissions on the Site Settings page.

3. Select Grant Permissions under the Permissions tab.

4. Type the name of the SharePoint group you wish to grant access to in the Share dialogue box.

5. The statement Invite others to Edit or Invite people with Can edit rights is displayed by default in the Share dialogue. This gives the SharePoint Members group permissions. To select a different permission level, click Show Choices, then click Select a permission level or Select a group or permission level to select a different SharePoint group or permission level. Groups and individual permission levels, such as Edit or View Only, are displayed in the dropdown box.

6. Press Share.

Delete a group

WARNING: Since deleting any of the default SharePoint groups could cause the system to become unstable, we advise against doing so. Only groups that you have formed and no longer wish to use should be deleted.

1. Click Settings, followed by Site Settings, on your Team Site or webpage.
2. Click People and Groups under Users and Permissions on the Site Settings page.
3. Click the name of the SharePoint group you wish to delete in the Quick Launch.
4. Select Group Settings after selecting Settings.
5. Click Delete on the Change Group Settings page's bottom.
6. Click OK in the confirmation window.

Assign a new permission level to a group.

You can assign a permission level that you've modified or made a new permission level to users or groups.

1. Click Settings, followed by Site Settings, on your team website.
2. Click Site Permissions under Users and Permissions on the Site Settings page.
3. Check the box next to the person or Group you wish to give the new permission level.
4. Select Edit User Permissions under the Permissions tab.
5. Check the box next to the name of the new permission level on the Edit Permissions screen. If you choose multiple levels of permission, the permission level that is allocated to the Group is the sum of each level's unique permissions. In other words, the new level for the Group includes permissions (A, B, C, D) if one level has permissions (A, B, C) and the other level includes permissions (C, D).
6. Click

Add, change, or remove a site collection administrator

1. Click Settings, followed by Site Settings, on your team website or blog.
2. Click Site Collection Administrators on the Site Settings page's Users and Permissions section.
3. Choose one of the following actions in the Site Collection Administrators box.
4. Enter the person's name or user alias to add them as a site collection administrator.
5. Click the X next to the name of the current site collection administrator, then type a new name.
6. Click the X next to the name of the site collection administrator to remove them.
7. Select OK.

NOTE: You must be a site collection administrator, a SharePoint Online administrator, or a global administrator in order to see the Site Collection Administrators link. Owners of the site are not able to see this link.

SETTING PERMISSIONS AND ACCESS LEVELS

The collection of permissions that permit users to carry out particular actions is referred to as default permission levels. When using the team site template, SharePoint Server is built to offer seven permission levels. (Other website templates call for more rights)

- **View-only permissions**: Viewing of application pages is permitted, and it is utilized just for Excel services. Users can browse information, view things, and more.

- Read permissions: Read permissions enables users to browse, list, and download goods and documents.

- **SharePoint edit permissions:** Users have access to manage and edit lists and documents in SharePoint.

- **Design permissions:** enables users to customize pages, apply themes, borders, and style sheets, as well as Edit, add, delete, and approve pages.

- **Limited access:** Users who have limited access are given fine-grained permissions to access shared and restricted resources, a particular asset, a document library, or a folder. The entire website cannot be accessed, edited, or deleted by users.

- **SharePoint contributes permissions:** Users can change personal views, manage objects, delete, update, and add user information, document libraries, directories, user information, and more with the use of SharePoint's contribute rights.

- **Full control:** Users are given complete control over the website and its permissions.

IMPLEMENTING INFORMATION RIGHTS MANAGEMENT (IRM)

By prohibiting users from printing or storing file copies, Information Rights Management (IRM) policies in SharePoint Online protect sensitive data from unauthorized access. Office products, including Word, Excel, PowerPoint, PDF, and XPS files, can all use IRM.

Turning on Rights Management in the Microsoft 365 Admin Centre

In contrast to SharePoint On-premises, IRM is pre-loaded in Office 365. Therefore, no additional software needs to be installed. The scope of IRM settings is at the list or library level. Before applying IRM to a SharePoint library or list, you must first activate the Information Rights Management Service for the organization through the Office 365 admin center. Activate IRM in Office 365 by doing the following steps:

 i. Open the Microsoft Admin Centre and log in.

 ii. Click on "Microsoft Azure Information Protection" after expanding Settings in the left navigation.

 iii. Make sure Rights management is turned on by selecting "Manage Microsoft Azure Information Protection settings" from the menu.

Through Azure Active Directory Rights Management, which is a part of the E3 and E4 plans, Office 365 offers IRM service

CHAPTER 7

STREAMLINING SHAREPOINT

SharePoint assists in managing company papers, records, media assets, and web content throughout all phases of their lifecycles, from creation to archiving, as a content management system.

CONFIGURING AND CUSTOMIZING SEARCH

The search tools of SharePoint are both powerful and versatile, and they can be configured to meet a wide range of needs imposed by organizations. This includes the ability to build and configure result sources, change the appearance of search results, and customize search schemas. In addition to this, SharePoint users have the option of receiving search query suggestions, which helps to improve the overall functionality of the search feature. SharePoint gives users the ability to personalize the Search Centre, which is a webpage dedicated to conducting searches and displaying the results of such searches.

At two distinct levels—the site level and the global admin (tAdmin) level—you have the ability to modify the SharePoint Search Results or switch the search choices that are displayed.

Setting up Search Options at the Site Level in Location 1

1. Go to Site Information by clicking the Gear Icon.
2. Go to Site Settings and click View All.
3. Choose Configure search settings from the Microsoft Settings section on the following page.
4. This will take you to a page where you may view some site-specific search statistics (insights).
5. Verticals and Result Types are two of the few movable choices at the top of the page.
6. You can change the Vertical tabs that are displayed at the top of the SharePoint Search Results Page by choosing the Verticals tab. These tabs aid in sorting results according to various types (such as Files, Sites, and Images). Both custom Verticals and the default Verticals can be edited.
7. You can configure Result kinds by choosing the Result Kinds tab. These enable you to change how search results are presented and organized on SharePoint Search Results Pages.

Setting up Search at the Global (Tenant) Level at Location 2

1. Select Admin frAdmine Microsoft 365 App Launcher menu.
2. Select All admin centers from the list of admin centers.
3. Select Search & Intel Admin Centre.
4. You'll see Insights (Search metrics), which is similar to the site-level version but this time includes metrics for the entire tenant rather than just one particular SharePoint site.
5. There are various analytics-related choices under the Insights Tab.
6. You can advertise particular results and respond to the most typical questions users could ask by using the Answers tab.
7. You can incorporate more sources into SharePoint search using the Data Sources tab. To enable searching of their material from SharePoint, for example, you may connect a CRM application or other third-party databases and applications.
8. You can change Verticals and Result Types on the Customizations tab (just like at the site level). This time around, the modifications are made to the entire tenant (Org-wide search), though.
9. Additional customization choices are available on the Configurations Tab, including the option to make SharePoint search results visible in Bing web search.

CONTENT MANAGEMENT IN SHAREPOINT

SharePoint Enterprise Content Management makes it easier to control and administer content that is located on an intranet. An organization as a whole will see improvements in its workflow, as well as its teamwork and collaboration. When it comes to effective content management, Microsoft Content Management System is the way to go, especially if you are already using other tools from Microsoft 365.

The SharePoint Content Management System (CMS) is an example of a headless CMS. This is done in order to maintain the separation between the content repository and the content display or interface. Because of the fragmented nature of the CMS, it is not necessary for users to have any prior technical knowledge in order to utilize it. Using the CMS appears to be straightforward because users do not need to be concerned about what is occurring in the background.

SharePoint does a fantastic job of effectively organizing and displaying content in a variety of formats. Users of SharePoint are granted the ability to rapidly create, manage, and distribute material thanks to the presence of libraries, lists, pages, and sites. The administration of structured data can be accomplished through the use of lists, and document libraries can be utilized for the storage, organization, and collaboration of files. While pages provide a framework for the presentation of material, sites make it possible to collect related assets in a centralized location. SharePoint also provides access to more sophisticated tools for the administration of material, such as workflows, versioning, and content types.

Create a Document Library

- Navigate to your SharePoint site and select "New" > "Document Library" from the dropdown menu.
- Give the library a name and provide a description if you want to.

Upload files and arrange them.

- In the document library, navigate to the "New" menu and select "File" or "Folder" from the dropdown menu.
- If necessary, upload files and folders or create new ones.

Sharing and working together on documents

- To share a document, right-click it and select the "Share" option.
- Enter the names or email addresses of the persons with whom you want to share, and then configure the permissions for that sharing.

TAGGING AND METADATA MANAGEMENT

SharePoint is equipped with robust tools that allow for the simultaneous management of metadata and tags. Users have the opportunity to tag content with relevant keywords, which makes it significantly easier to arrange and discover the information later on. Metadata, which is data that describes other data, may also be managed pretty effectively in SharePoint. Metadata is data that describes data. The metadata associated with a document can contain a variety of details, some of which include the author of the document, the date it was created, and even more information. SharePoint's managed metadata service makes it possible to establish hierarchical groups of keywords that are centralized and can be used across the entirety of an organization. This functionality is made available through the platform's content management system.

Create a Managed Metadata Column

- Navigate to the list or library you have created in SharePoint, and then click on the "Add column" and then the "More" option.
- Choose "Managed Metadata" from the dropdown menu in the new column dialogue box.

Configure the Metadata Column

- Give the column a name, and then adjust the settings.
- Choose a term set that will be associated with the column to be displayed.

RECORDS MANAGEMENT AND COMPLIANCE

SharePoint is equipped with features for maintaining records, which guarantees that important documents are kept safe and can be recovered whenever they are required. This means that important documents can be accessed whenever they are required. Records in SharePoint are immutable, which means that once they have been declared, they cannot be altered in any way. This applies to both read-only and editable records. SharePoint also provides retention policies, which specify how long a record should be kept and after what amount of time it should be removed. These policies may be found in the "Administrative Centre."

SharePoint contains capabilities that can assist firms in conforming to regulations, and these capabilities can be found in SharePoint. This includes data loss prevention skills, the eDiscovery capabilities for discovering content in electronic format, and the auditing capabilities for keeping track of operations. These capabilities help to ensure that SharePoint's content is managed in a manner that satisfies the appropriate regulatory and legal requirements, thereby contributing to SharePoint's reputation for compliance.

1. Enable In-Place Records Management
   - Open the SharePoint Admin Centre on your web browser.
   - Select "More features" and then "Record declaration settings" from the dropdown menu.
2. Configure Record Declaration Settings
   - Determine which options for the record declaration work best for your requirements.
   - Save your modifications.

3. Apply Retention Labels

- Navigate to a document library or list hosted on SharePoint.
- Choose a document or item to label, then click the information icon, and finally click the "Apply label" button.
- Select the appropriate label for the retention period.

CHAPTER 8

INTEGRATING SHAREPOINT WITH OTHER TOOLS

SharePoint may be integrated with a wide range of apps, allowing users to fulfill their objectives of simplifying workflows, boosting productivity, and creating a unified digital workplace. The following is a list of tools that are regularly integrated with SharePoint, along with the methods that are necessary to do so:

INTEGRATION WITH MICROSOFT OFFICE SUITE

You will be able to boost the effectiveness of your work processes as well as the amount of collaboration you have with your team if you connect SharePoint with the Microsoft Office Suite. This will be achievable for you if you make the connection. In order to accomplish this task for some of the more prevalent Office apps, you can do it in the following manner:

The Microsoft Office suite, including Word, Excel, PowerPoint, and OneNote

Because Microsoft SharePoint is directly integrated with these programs, you will be able to open and save files immediately to SharePoint without any additional steps.

1. Launch a program from Microsoft Office, such as Word, Excel, PowerPoint, or OneNote.
2. To open or save the file, depending on what you want to do, select "Open" or "Save As" from the "File" menu in the top-left corner of the screen.
3. Depending on the version of Office you are using, select "SharePoint Sites" or "Sites - Your Company Name" from the dropdown menu.
4. Within SharePoint, navigate to the location where you wish to open or save your file, and then click there.

Syncing with OneDrive:

Integration between SharePoint and Microsoft's cloud storage platform OneDrive, known simply as OneDrive, is now a possibility. Users are given the ability to synchronize SharePoint libraries on their local machines and continue working on data even if they are unable to connect to the internet. This enables users to make the most of their time spent working with SharePoint. Any edits that were made to SharePoint while the user was disconnected from the internet are saved there as soon as they are reconnected to the internet by SharePoint.

Integration with Outlook:

As a result of SharePoint's connection with Microsoft Outlook, users now have the ability to subscribe to RSS feeds from SharePoint sites within Outlook, share documents with one another through the use of email, and synchronize SharePoint calendars with their personal calendars.

CONNECTING SHAREPOINT WITH OUTLOOK AND ONEDRIVE

Integration with Outlook

A streamlined and efficient workspace is produced whenever SharePoint and Outlook are connected to one another in any way. This is made possible by integrating a wide range of resources and technologies onto a single platform. This is accomplished by enabling users to access SharePoint calendars, task lists, and document libraries directly from within the user interface of their Outlook client. Both teamwork and communication will benefit from this change. Because of this integration, it is now able to keep everyone on the team up to date in real-time with changes that are made to shared calendars, properly manage documents, and interact with no issues at all. Users are also able to remain within the familiar constraints of their Outlook environment, which helps to increase productivity by reducing the amount of time spent jumping between different applications. This integration, in the end, results in an improved workflow, which, in turn, leads to increased productivity and improved communication within the team.

I will now walk you through the steps on how to sync a SharePoint calendar to Outlook so that you can view your appointments in Outlook. This sync will allow you to access your appointments in SharePoint. You would repeat these steps in exactly the same order in order to synchronize other SharePoint web parts to Outlook, such as contacts, tasks, and so on.

Proceed to the web page that contains the component that you wish to sync with Outlook.

1. Launch Microsoft Outlook, and then navigate to the calendar view within the program.
2. Click "Home" followed by "Open Calendar" and then "From Address Book..."
3. Conduct a search for the calendar in SharePoint that you wish to add, select it, and then click the "OK" button.
4. To connect a list in SharePoint to Outlook, do the following:
5. Go to the SharePoint list that you want to connect with Outlook, and then navigate to it.
6. Navigate to the List tab, and within the "Connect & Export" group, click the "Connect to Outlook" button.
7. A window will go up asking you to confirm that you are comfortable letting the website launch an application on your computer. Simply select the "Allow" option.

8. Another popup will display, this time asking you whether you want to link Outlook to the SharePoint list. Tap the "Yes" button.

Integrating with OneDrive

Integration between SharePoint and Microsoft's cloud storage platform OneDrive, known simply as OneDrive, is now a possibility. Users are given the opportunity to synchronize SharePoint libraries on their local machines and to continue working on data even when they are not connected to the internet. This capacity is made available to users through a feature that is built into SharePoint. Any edits performed by the user while they were disconnected from the internet are immediately uploaded to SharePoint when they re-establish their connection to the internet.

THIRD-PARTY INTEGRATIONS AND ADD-ONS

Connecting the products that employees regularly use to SharePoint can assist in streamlining workflows that involve these products. Whether or not this is something that should be done depends on the goals that you want to achieve.

Methods and Programs for the Management of Relationships with Clients

The ability of SharePoint to interface with customer relationship management (CRM) systems simplifies the handling of paperwork associated with marketing and sales activities. CRM stands for "customer relationship management." The process of filling out proposals, contracts, or agreements typically takes time and requires great attention to be paid to the specifics of the information being entered. The integration of SharePoint and CRM enables sales and marketing teams to automatically import CRM data into document templates anytime a new document for a client needs to be prepared. This may be done whenever there is a need to generate a new document. Both teams will benefit from this huge time savings as a result. As a direct result of this, the process of creating papers is sped up, and errors are eliminated. Users of CRM have the option of saving papers on SharePoint as well. This not only frees up storage space within CRM but also reduces the costs associated with CRM storage and offers version control for the documents.

The "enterprise resource planning."

When integrated with enterprise resource planning (ERP) software, SharePoint adds value and makes it simpler to manage distributed data from an organization's various stakeholders. Invoices, delivery slips, and receipts, for example, can be uploaded by a company's partner or customer to SharePoint, where they will be automatically recognized, parsed, and then transferred to the proper folders in an ERP system. SharePoint is able to do this because ERP systems are designed to recognize and parse structured data.

Various Approaches to the Planning of Human Resources

The integration of SharePoint with HR planning tools ensures that the necessary staff will always have access to the most current and correct information at the right moments. SharePoint, when integrated with an HR management system, grants employees customized access to the records that are relevant to them. This empowers employees to do their jobs more effectively. The employees are able to make changes to their personal information, conduct performance reviews, view and book annual leave, and view their payslips on the intranet, for example. In addition, they can view their annual leave options.

IT Helpdesks

It is much simpler for users of an IT helpdesk that is connected to SharePoint to provide themselves with self-service choices and speed up the process of problem resolution for themselves. SharePoint gives employees the option to use pre-populated forms and the capability to quickly create helpdesk tickets with acceptable issue descriptions. Additionally, employees now have access to pre-populated forms. Employees are also able to track the advancement of their own support cases within SharePoint, which is a benefit to the company. When linked together, SharePoint and IT helpdesks make it feasible for IT specialists to develop guides for employees and synchronize knowledge bases. Both of these functions may be performed more efficiently.

Digital Asset Management Systems

It is a time-consuming procedure that entails searching for and uploading relevant media assets from a digital asset management (DAM) system in order to make news, presentations, and other materials that will be shared within an intranet. This process is necessary in order to develop materials that will be shared within the organization. SharePoint is an application that, when combined with a digital asset management system, makes it considerably simpler to distribute and manage content.

Different Ways of Fitting Everything Together

You can swiftly expand SharePoint thanks to the expandability characteristics that it possesses. This allows you to do things like send data and files that are kept in an intranet to other systems or add data from other sources to SharePoint. If a third-party system is able to accept integrations, it is usually possible to link it to an internal SharePoint network, which is one of the benefits of using SharePoint. When the SharePoint Framework (SPFx) is used, the SharePoint connection Services make it easy to leverage ready-made connectors and develop unique connection scenarios. This is made possible by the fact that the SharePoint Framework was built on top of.NET.

Approaches and Methods That Are Integrated

When an organization has to integrate SharePoint with another system, they can do so in a variety of ways, depending on the kind of system they need to integrate SharePoint with and the resources they have available to them.

Connectors

Whenever there is a demand for SharePoint to be merged with a well-known product that is not part of the Microsoft 365 family, it is advisable to seek out accessible connectors on Microsoft AppSource. This may be done whenever there is a need to do so. In the case that a pre-built application is not acceptable for an organization's needs, the organization has the option of commissioning the construction of a bespoke connector for internal use in the event that this is more appropriate.

Microsoft Power Platform

Within the Microsoft 365 ecosystem, the tools for analyzing data, automating workflows, and building new apps based on data and processes are consolidated under the Microsoft Power Platform. These tools may be accessed through the Microsoft 365 portal. The Power Platform is a collection of several useful technologies that are brought together in order to simplify the process of establishing connectivity across the many products that are part of the Microsoft 365 suite. SharePoint is one of these products that we offer. To ensure that companies are able to reap the benefits of the products and data offered by the Power Platform, Microsoft mandates that these companies purchase a license for the Power Platform from the company.

The Capability of Automating

Utilizing Power Automate allows for the workflows of SharePoint and a wide number of other apps to be automatically and completely automated. More than 300 distinct data sources can be brought together using Power Automate. This number does not only include programs that are part of Microsoft 365; it also includes applications from third-party companies that are not included in Microsoft 365.

Power BI

Power BI is a tool that not only takes data from the underlying data platform of the Microsoft Power Platform but also from other applications that are part of MS 365. The Microsoft Power Platform provides access to these data at your convenience. The data that was collected may be accessed using an application called Power BI. However, with the assistance of a specialized web element, it is also feasible to publish the data in SharePoint and store bespoke reports within the private network of an enterprise.

Apps that Pack a Punch

Power Apps is a set of tools that allows users to swiftly develop a bespoke business application and connect it to a range of data sources, including the lists and libraries that are stored in SharePoint. This capacity is made possible by a suite of tools known as Power Apps. SharePoint can also act as a document repository for apps of this kind, which is another useful capacity it possesses.

Enhance Your Productivity Using the Software

SharePoint is a platform that is straightforward to incorporate with many other types of software. You can connect it with software that is readily accessible off-the-shelf, or that was designed expressly for your organization, and then you can reap the benefits of the synergy that it provides.

CHAPTER 9

SHAREPOINT ONLINE AND OFFICE 365

In the quickly developing digital landscape of today, businesses are increasingly relying on collaboration tools and cloud-based platforms to streamline their operations and enhance their productivity in order to keep up with the competition. Both Microsoft SharePoint Online and Office 365 are powerful technologies that offer seamless integration, which enables businesses to improve their skills in the areas of communication, collaboration, and information management. In this chapter, we will investigate SharePoint Online, look into the capabilities and advantages of integrating Office 365, and talk about the process of moving to SharePoint Online.

UNDERSTANDING SHAREPOINT ONLINE

Microsoft's Office 365 comes with a platform called SharePoint Online, which is hosted in the cloud. SharePoint Online is offered by Microsoft. Documents, files, and information can be stored, organized, shared, and worked on collaboratively by several users inside the same organization thanks to the centralized hub that it provides. SharePoint Online makes it possible for teams to collaborate effectively, regardless of where in the world they are physically located, by simplifying access to resources and enhancing the quality of their communication.

The adaptability and scalability of SharePoint Online are one of the platform's most significant strengths. Intranet portals, team sites, and sites for managing projects are all examples of the types of websites that may be created using SharePoint and then customized to match the specific needs of the organization. SharePoint Online also provides a wide variety of built-in features, such as document version control, metadata tagging, and search capabilities, which make it simpler to locate and manage content. SharePoint Online is available in both on-premises and cloud-based deployments.

FEATURES AND BENEFITS OF OFFICE 365 INTEGRATION

The integration of Office 365 integrates the powerful collaborative capabilities of SharePoint Online along with additional productivity tools made by Microsoft, including Word, Excel, PowerPoint, and Outlook. This connection provides a number of features and benefits, which collectively improve the quality of the user experience and the effectiveness of the company.

Effortless Collaboration:

Users are able to edit documents simultaneously, keep track of changes, and interact in real time, thanks to the incorporation of Office 365. Because of this, the working atmosphere becomes more effective and productive, and members of the team are better able to contribute to projects and work together without friction.

Improved Communication:

Outlook, Teams, and Yammer are just a few of the different communication tools that are included in Office 365. Within the confines of the SharePoint environment, users are able to connect with one another, share information, and discuss the status of their projects while using these tools because they can be integrated with SharePoint Online.

Accessibility via Mobile Devices:

Users are able to access and update documents regardless of where they are by utilizing mobile-friendly features built into both Office 365 and SharePoint Online. Employees are able to maintain their connection to the company and continue their productive work even when they are away from the office, thanks to mobile apps that are available for both iOS and Android.

Comprehensive Protection and Compliance:

Office 365 provides users with sophisticated security safeguards, which protect sensitive data and guarantee the software is compliant with industry laws. As a result of

SharePoint Online's seamless integration with these security safeguards, businesses can feel confident in their ability to share and collaborate on critical documents without compromising their data security.

Scalability and effectiveness in terms of cost:

Office 365 is a subscription-based service, which means that businesses can adjust the amount of software they use to correspond with their requirements. This removes the requirement for enterprises to make preliminary investments in infrastructure and enables more effective resource allocation inside the company.

MIGRATING TO SHAREPOINT ONLINE

It is necessary to carefully plan and carry out the migration to SharePoint Online when coming from an on-premises SharePoint setup or switching from another content management system. During the process of migrating, the following are some important steps to keep in mind:

Evaluating the Situation in Its Current Form:

An in-depth analysis of a company's current environment, including its content inventory, permissions, and customizations, should be performed prior to any migration efforts being undertaken by that business. This evaluation contributes to the process of assessing the magnitude and level of difficulty of the migration.

The Processes of Planning and Strategy:

It is recommended to work on putting together a thorough migration plan that details the goals, timetable, and distribution of resources. In order to achieve a seamless transition, it is essential to involve all of the relevant stakeholders as well as the end users, in the planning process.

The Process of Preparing the Content:

It is absolutely necessary to clean up and organize any existing content in order to maximize the effectiveness of the migrating process. In order to assist effective content management using SharePoint Online, it is necessary to get rid of any redundant, obsolete, or superfluous material and to properly tag any information that is stored.

Connecting the Dots Between Permissions and Security:

SharePoint Online operates under its own security and authorization paradigm, which may or may not be compatible with the one currently in place. In order to successfully complete the migration process, one of the most important steps is to map the n permissions and verify that users and groups have access to the right levels. It is absolutely necessary to do an analysis and bring the existing permission structure in line with the security framework of SharePoint Online.

Data Migration:

The actual transfer of material can be carried out in a number of different ways, depending on the quantity of data and the level of complexity involved. SharePoint Online provides users with a variety of choices, such as manually uploading content, utilizing tools for mass transfer, or relying on third-party migration solutions. Validating the migrated data and ensuring that its integrity is maintained throughout the process is absolutely necessary.

The Configuration and Personalization Process:

After the content has been moved, organizations need to configure SharePoint Online so that it satisfies the criteria that are unique to their business. This involves the process of establishing site structures, document libraries, processes, and any adaptations that may be required to recreate the functionality of the previous environment.

Adoption of Users and Instruction:

A seamless adoption of the new system by users is necessary for the success of the transfer. End users are far more likely to understand a new platform, its features, and how to make full use of the platform's capabilities if they are provided with extensive training and assistance. In addition, feedback from users ought to be actively sought out and responded to in order to improve the user experience.

Management and Governance on an Ongoing Basis:

In order to ensure that SharePoint Online will continue to be successful after the migration, it is absolutely necessary to develop governance policies and best practices. This comprises the definition of roles and duties, the implementation of version control, and the establishment of strategies for content lifecycle management. Maintaining the platform's security and functionality requires consistent monitoring and maintenance, as well as software updates.

SharePoint Online, when combined with Office 365, provides businesses of any size with a robust solution for facilitating collaboration as well as the management of information. Businesses have the ability to increase communication and workflows, as well as their overall productivity, by gaining a better understanding of the possibilities and benefits offered by SharePoint Online, which is also seamlessly integrated with the tools offered by Office 365.

Moving to SharePoint Online calls for extensive preparation in the form of planning, evaluation, and implementation. Organizations are able to successfully move their content while maintaining the integrity of their data and guaranteeing a smooth experience for their users if they follow a planned migration strategy and involve key stakeholders in the process.

The integration of SharePoint Online with Office 365 offers businesses a powerful platform on which they can improve their collaboration and content management procedures. By making use of the capabilities and advantages offered by this integration, organizations have the opportunity to improve their communication, streamline their processes, and cultivate a culture of cooperation, all of which ultimately contribute to increased productivity and success in the digital age.

CHAPTER 10

MASTERING SHAREPOINT

ESSENTIAL SHAREPOINT BEST PRACTICES

1. Establish a Clear Governance Plan

It is essential for your organization to build a governance plan prior to adopting SharePoint. This plan should define how the platform will be used and managed once it is deployed. This plan ought to contain things like user permissions, site creation policies, content management, and measures of security and compliance. Your SharePoint system may benefit from the implementation of a well-defined governance structure, which may help reduce the likelihood of confusion, guarantee consistency, and improve its overall efficiency.

2. Use Metadata and Site Columns

SharePoint's organization and searchability can both be improved with the use of metadata and site columns. Make advantage of metadata to tag and organize your content rather than depending entirely on folder structures to do so. Users will have an easier time finding the information they require, even if they are unaware of the location in which it is stored, as a result of this change. On the other hand, site columns encourage consistency by ensuring that the same metadata is utilized across a variety of different lists and libraries. This helps to avoid duplication of effort.

3. Leverage SharePoint's Versioning Capabilities

The versioning function of SharePoint enables users to maintain track of changes made to a document and, if necessary, revert back to an earlier version of the document. When working with complicated documents that go through a lot of different iterations, this tool can be an absolute godsend. It is important to keep in mind that there should be a cap placed on the number of versions that are kept in order to prevent excessive consumption of storage space.

4. Implement a Regular Backup and Recovery Plan

Despite the robust nature of SharePoint, it is still possible for data to be lost as a result of unintentional deletions, hardware failures, or other unanticipated occurrences. It is absolutely necessary to have a routine backup and recovery plan in order to secure your data and guarantee the continuity of your organization. Regular testing of your recovery methods is necessary to ensure that they perform as expected.

TIPS FOR EFFICIENT COLLABORATION IN SHAREPOINT

1. Utilize SharePoint Team Sites

Team Sites in SharePoint offer members of a team a centralized location in which they can manage projects, share information with one another, and collaborate on documents. Utilizing Team Sites can help strengthen team cohesion and make cooperation more efficient.

2. Co-Author Documents in Real Time

Because SharePoint enables many users to simultaneously make edits to a document, the practice of e-mailing document attachments back and forth becomes unnecessary. Through real-time cooperation, time can be saved, confusion can be reduced, and productivity may be increased.

3. Make use of the Workflows in SharePoint

SharePoint workflows provide the ability to automate a variety of procedures, including document approval and issue tracking processes, thereby lowering the amount of manual labor and the likelihood of errors. Workflows' efficacy and consistency can both be significantly improved by the automation of routine processes.

4. Make Use of Notifications for Updates

When there are modifications made to a document or list, SharePoint's alert feature will notify you of those changes. You may stay up to speed on changes and updates by setting up alerts, which can help you respond quickly to any shifts.

TROUBLESHOOTING COMMON SHAREPOINT ISSUES

1. Issues with the Capabilities of the Search Function

Check your metadata and the search settings if users are having problems discovering the stuff you've provided. Make sure that the content is classified appropriately, and check that the search configuration includes all sources that are pertinent. If the problem persists, you might want to consider re-indexing the content of your SharePoint site.

2. Problems with the Access Granted to Users

Access issues or potential security breaches may result from incorrectly configured user permissions. In order to guarantee that users have the appropriate amount of access, user permissions should be reviewed and updated on a regular basis. It is recommended that you make use of SharePoint groups in order to manage rights effectively.

3. Poor Overall Performance

If SharePoint is operating slowly, this may be the result of a number of different issues, including the presence of huge lists, heavy traffic, or insufficient server resources. Determine the root of the problem and think about potential solutions, such as improving the site's structure, adopting content archiving, or updating the infrastructure of your servers.

4. Difficulties with User-Defined Functions

Custom features have the potential to expand SharePoint's capabilities, but they also have the potential to create problems if they are not designed correctly. If a bespoke feature is the root of the issue, you should discuss the matter with the person responsible for developing the feature, or you might look into using pre-built features instead.

CHAPTER 11

FUTURE TRENDS AND DEVELOPMENTS IN SHAREPOINT

SharePoint is a significant player in the digital collaboration ecosystem, which is constantly shifting, and there are many new developments happening in this space. As we go deeper into anticipated developments and trends in SharePoint, it is imperative that we examine both the planned improvements and roadmap for SharePoint Online as well as the incorporation of emerging technologies into SharePoint.

SHAREPOINT ONLINE UPDATES AND ROADMAP

SharePoint's Enhanced Security Functions and Features

Microsoft is giving top priority to the development of improvements to the security capabilities of SharePoint Online, which will turn it into a platform that is more resistant to the possibility of cyberattacks. The incorporation of a Web Application Firewall (also known as WAF) is one of the most important aspects of these enhancements. The Web Application Firewall (WAF) is intended to provide an additional layer of protection by monitoring HTTP traffic and preventing risks from connecting to the server. Because of the effectiveness of this safeguard against SQL injections, Cross-Site Scripting (XSS), and DDoS attacks, data, and applications hosted on SharePoint Online are protected from harm.

Constant Improvements to Both the User Experience and the Safety of the System:

Microsoft often releases updates with the intention of enhancing both the quality of the user experience and the level of security. These changes include the implementation of robust, one-of-a-kind passwords for each account, the installation of regular security patches, the establishment of secure data connections, and the deployment of security plugins.

Additional Precautions to Take for Your Safety:

Microsoft is releasing a number of new features, most of which are geared toward improving the company's security. Two-factor authentication (2FA), regular backups, monitoring of SharePoint, restrictions on file uploads, secure file transfer protocol (FTP), parameterized queries, and turning off file editing from the dashboard are some of these precautions.

Putting an Emphasis on Education for the Users:

Microsoft places a strong emphasis on the need for user education regarding security best practices in order to ensure that the SharePoint Online environment is kept safe. This is a component of their holistic security strategy.

EMERGING TECHNOLOGIES AND SHAREPOINT

The score for Office 365's Security:

This cutting-edge solution gives enterprises the ability to comprehend and improve their security posture by providing reporting and insights pertaining to security.

The Information Protection and Compliance Team at Microsoft:

Designed from the ground up to provide organizations with specialized assistance in satisfying complex compliance, privacy, and secrecy requirements.

ATP stands for Advanced Threat Protection.

An important new feature will be added to SharePoint with the intention of defending companies and other organizations from malicious assaults by detecting, investigating, and providing specific information about those attacks.

Customer Lockbox is available for use with Office 365:

Because of this feature, you can be assured that a support engineer from Microsoft will only access your files when it is necessary and with your prior consent.

Security for Office 365 Cloud Applications:

This tool improves insight into your cloud apps and services, providing advanced analytics to help identify and combat potential cyber-attacks.

Office 365 Advanced Security Management includes the following:

A tool that can monitor actions taking place within an organization's Office 365 environment and detect any potential security breaches.

CONCLUSION

In the early chapters of this book, we ventured to understand what SharePoint is, delving into its core components and functionalities. From there, we navigated through the complexities of its setup while also exploring its integration potential with the broader Microsoft Office Suite. Throughout this journey, I hope that you've not only learned how to work around potential roadblocks but also discovered the true potential that SharePoint holds in transforming your workspaces and enhancing your collaborative efforts.

One of the beautiful facets of SharePoint is its adaptability, its ability to grow, learn, and morph into better versions of itself to cater to evolving needs and technologies. I hope that as SharePoint continues to evolve, you, too, will keep pace, embracing the changes and the continuous learning process that comes with it.

If there's one crucial takeaway from this book, it is this - SharePoint, in its dynamic and expansive essence, is not a tool to be feared or avoided. Instead, it is a platform brimming with potential, waiting to be harnessed. It can simplify your work, streamline your processes, and empower you to create, share, and collaborate more efficiently and effectively.

Throughout these pages, we've embarked on a journey of discovery, exploration, and, hopefully, a sense of mastery. But remember, the end of this book is not the end of your SharePoint journey; rather, it is a launchpad, a solid foundation from which you can continue building your understanding and expertise.

Whether you're a seasoned professional or someone just stepping into the world of Microsoft SharePoint, remember that each day presents a new opportunity to learn, grow, and explore the limitless potential that SharePoint offers.

As we wrap up this journey together, I wish to express my gratitude for having me as your guide. It has been an honor, and I am genuinely excited to see where your SharePoint journey leads you. In the world of technology, change is the only constant, and the only limits that exist are the ones we set for ourselves.

So, continue to learn, continue to explore. Technology is our ally, here to aid us, not intimidate us. Today, you've mastered SharePoint. Tomorrow, who knows what new frontiers you'll conquer?

Wishing you all the best in your ongoing journey of exploration, knowledge, and mastery,

Made in the USA
Monee, IL
17 June 2024

59954213R00079